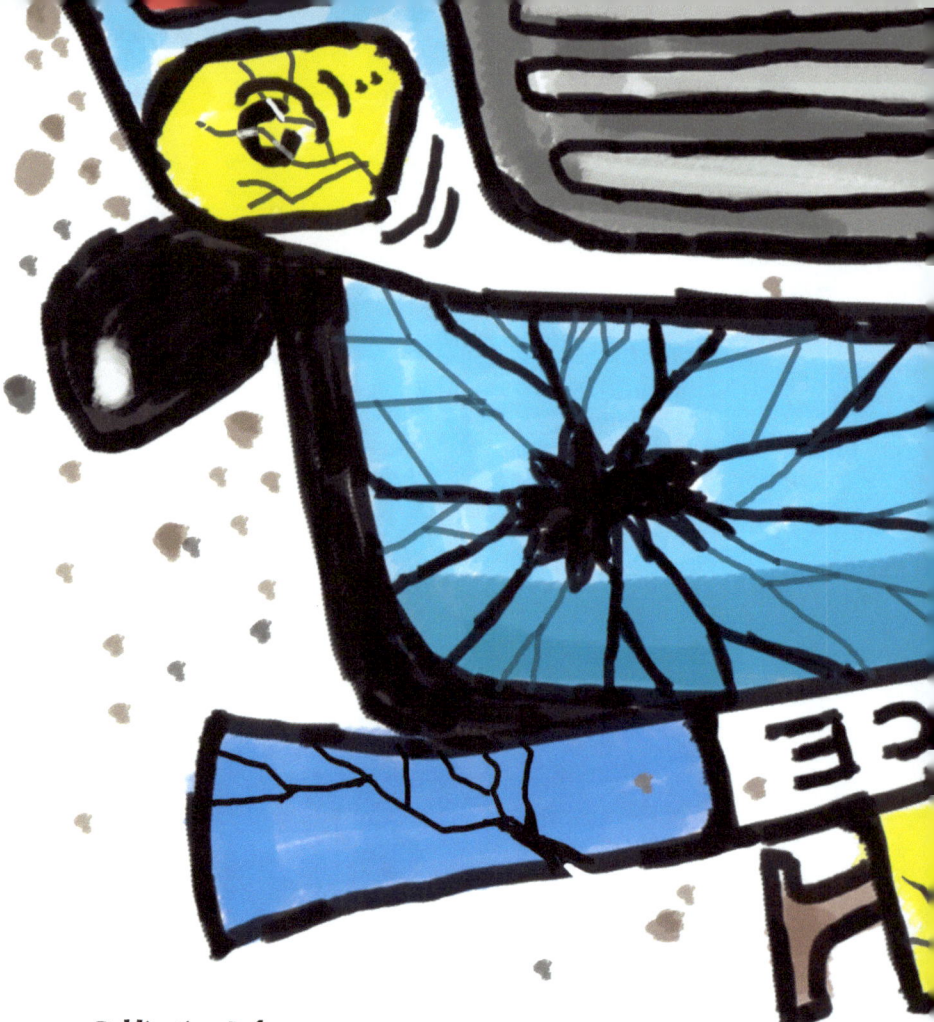

Publication Info:
Author: Ricardo Sosa
Art By: Charbak Dipta
Editor: Kristina Phu
Final Layout Design: Josie Lanuza

This book or any portion thereof may not be reproduced or used in any manner whatsoever without the express written permission of the publisher except for the use of brief quotations in a book review.

Printed in the United States of America
ISBN: 978-1-7371332-1-6
First Printing, 2021

Copyright © 2021 by Ricardo Sosa. All rights reserved.
www.efftwelve.world

Library of Congress Control Number: 2021941762

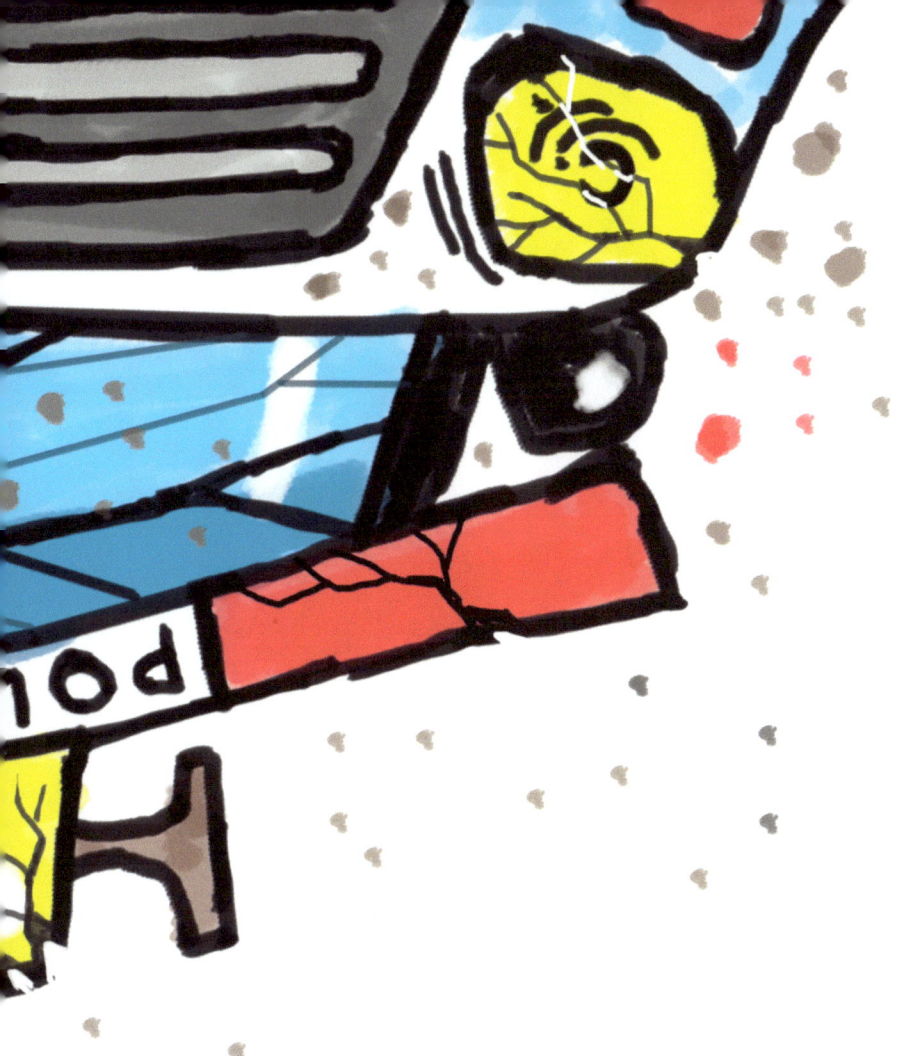

EFF TWELVE

THE HOMIES GUIDE TO DEALING WITH 12

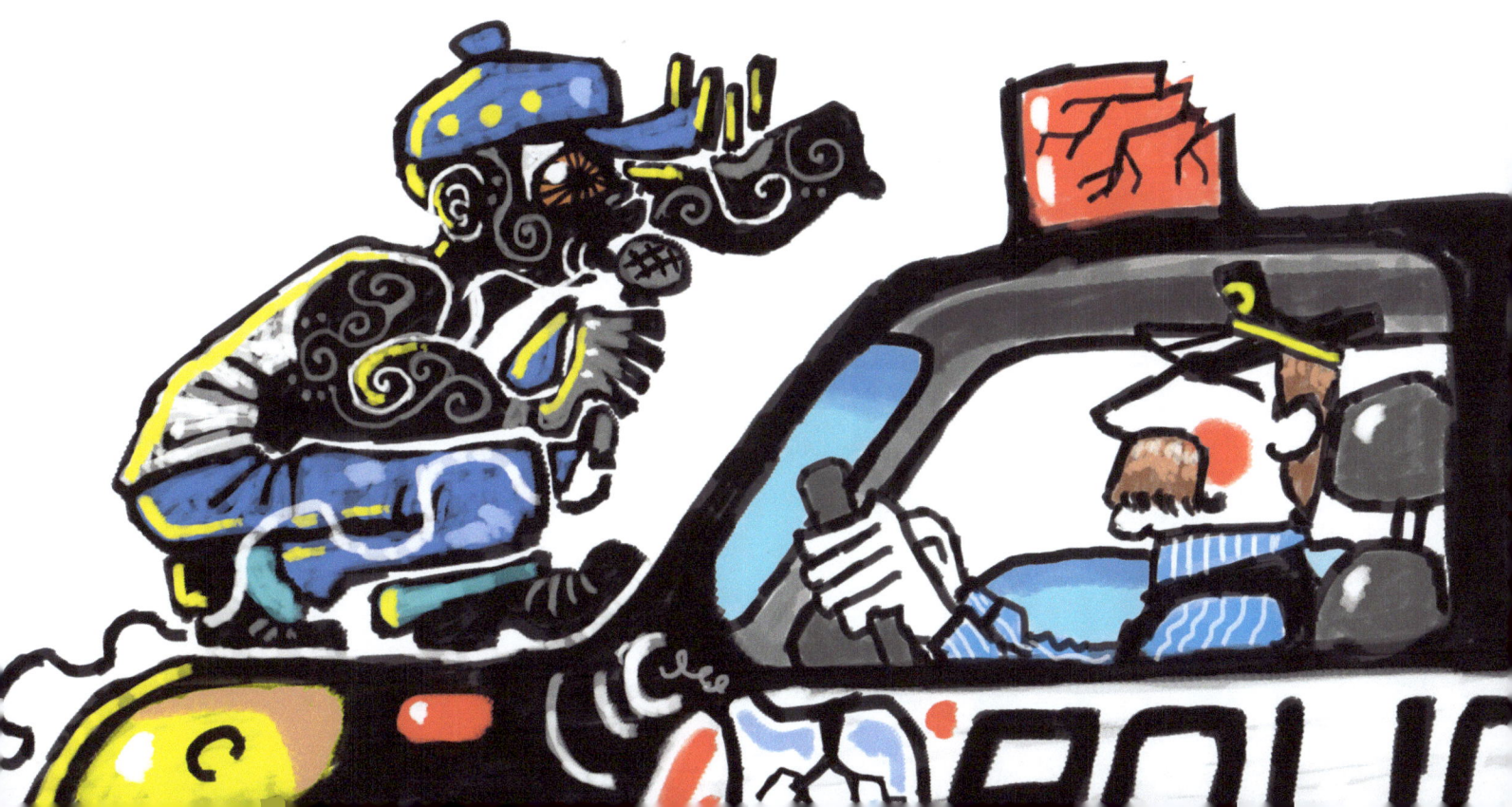

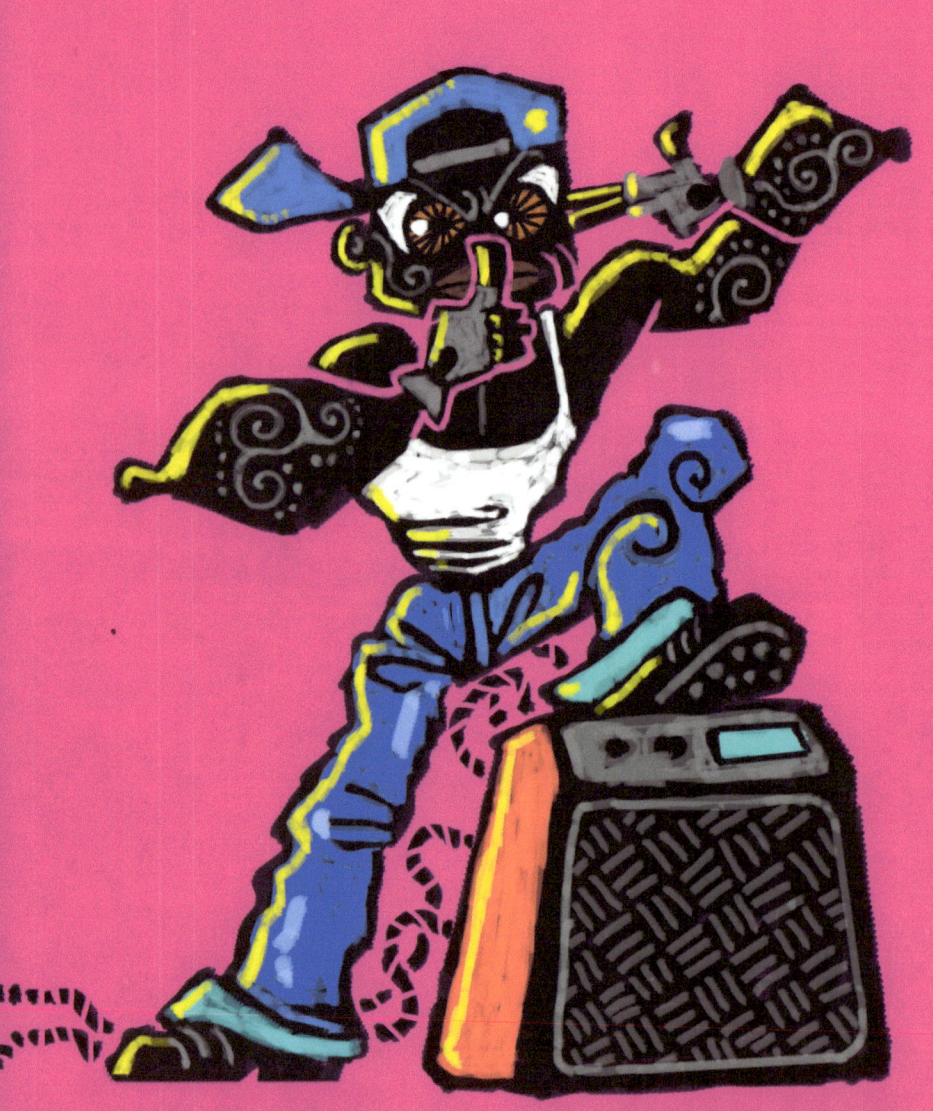

DISCLAIMER

FYI, **I AM NOT A LAWYER**.

THIS BOOK IS NOT INTENDED AS A SUBSTITUTE FOR LEGAL ADVICE.

THE READER SHOULD DO THEIR OWN RESEARCH AND CONSULT WITH A LAWYER OR POLICE, IN MATTERS RELATING TO HIS OR HER PERSONAL SITUATION.

I INTENDED FOR Y'ALL TO ONLY USE THIS INFORMATION AS A 'GUIDE'.

*ANY SLANG WORD YOU MAY NOT UNDERSTAND CAN BE FOUND IN THE GLOSSARY IN THE BACK OF THE BOOK

AUTHOR'S NOTE

HEY, WHAT'S UP HOMIES! FIRST AND FOREMOST, I WOULD LIKE TO THANK Y'ALL FOR BEING A PART OF THIS BOOK.

THE MAIN PURPOSE WAS TO BRING AWARENESS TO THE RIGHTS THAT WE POSSESS AS CITIZENS. TOO OFTEN, MINORITIES ARE BEING KILLED BY TWELVE FOR NO REASON BECAUSE THEY TAKE THE LAW INTO THEIR OWN HANDS. THIS SPARKED A FIRE IN ME TO FIND A CREATIVE WAY FOR YOU TO INGEST AND LEARN OUR CIVIL LIBERTIES BECAUSE BEING AN INFORMED CITIZEN CAN POTENTIALLY SAVE YOUR LIFE.

I AM HOPING THAT WITH THIS INFORMATION, WE WILL BE ABLE TO GET HOME SAFE TO OUR FAMILIES AFTER AN ENCOUNTER WITH TWELVE.

SIDENOTE: REMEMBER, NOT ALL TWELVE ARE BAD.

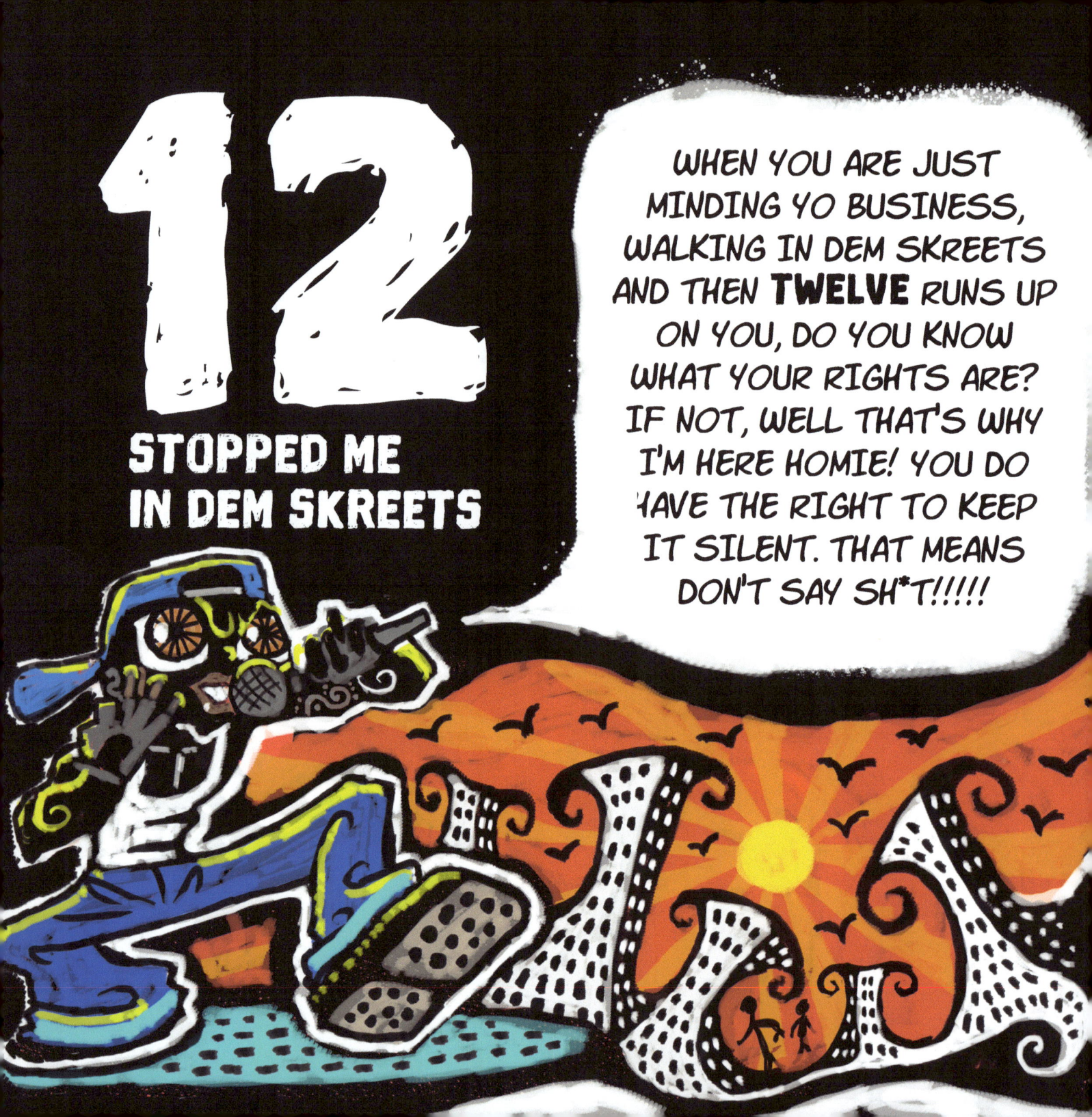

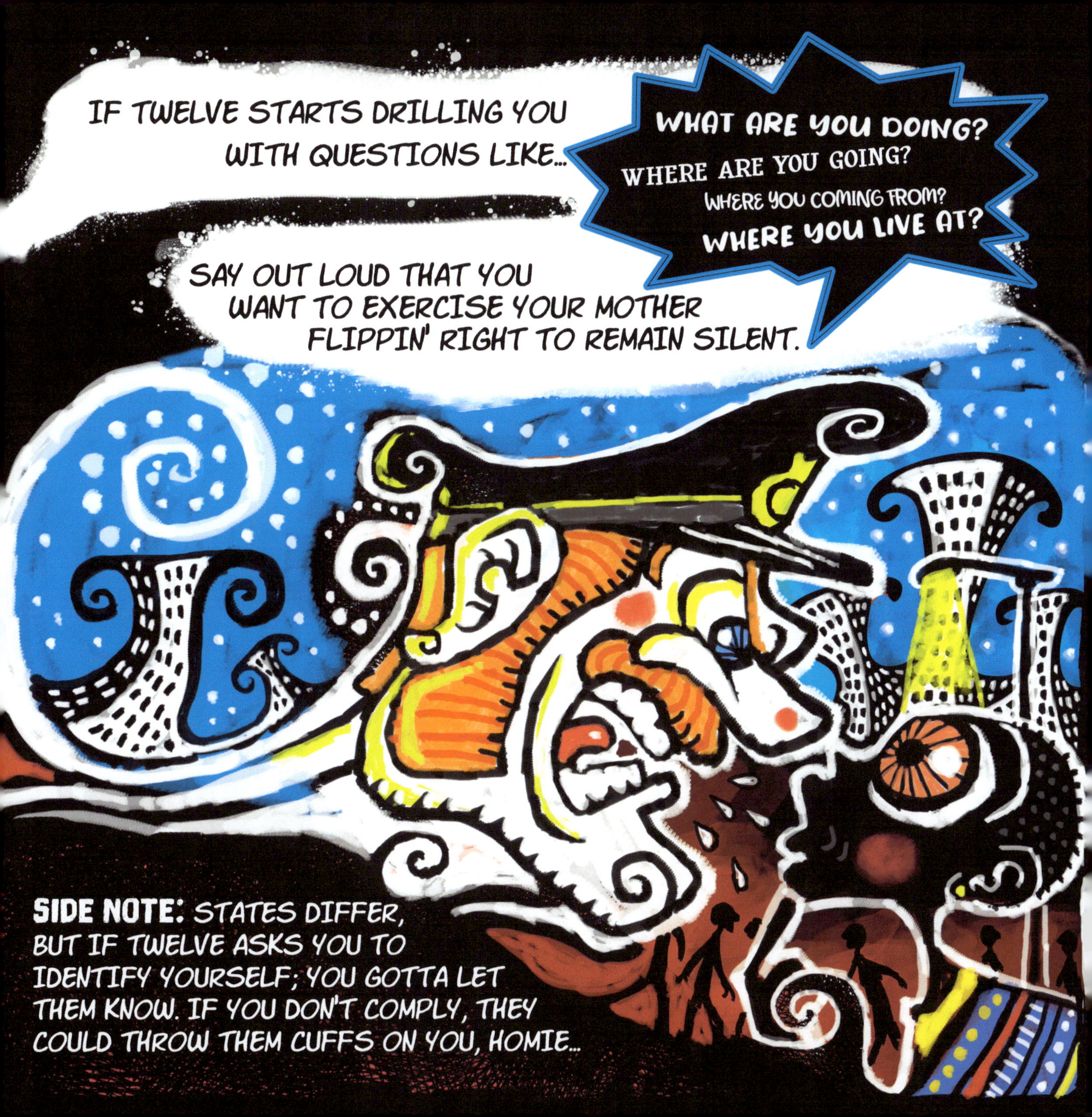

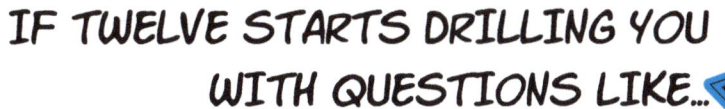

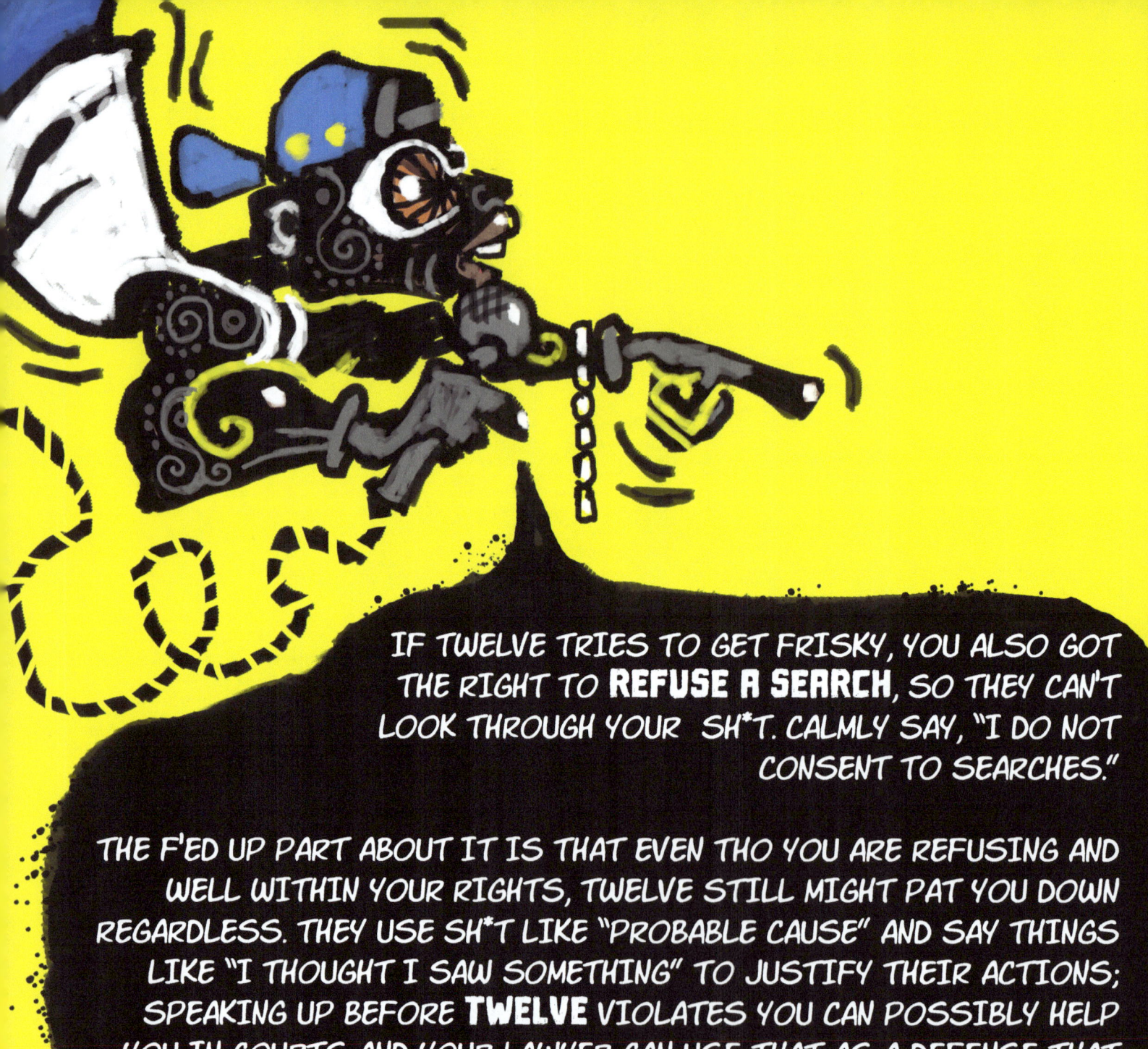

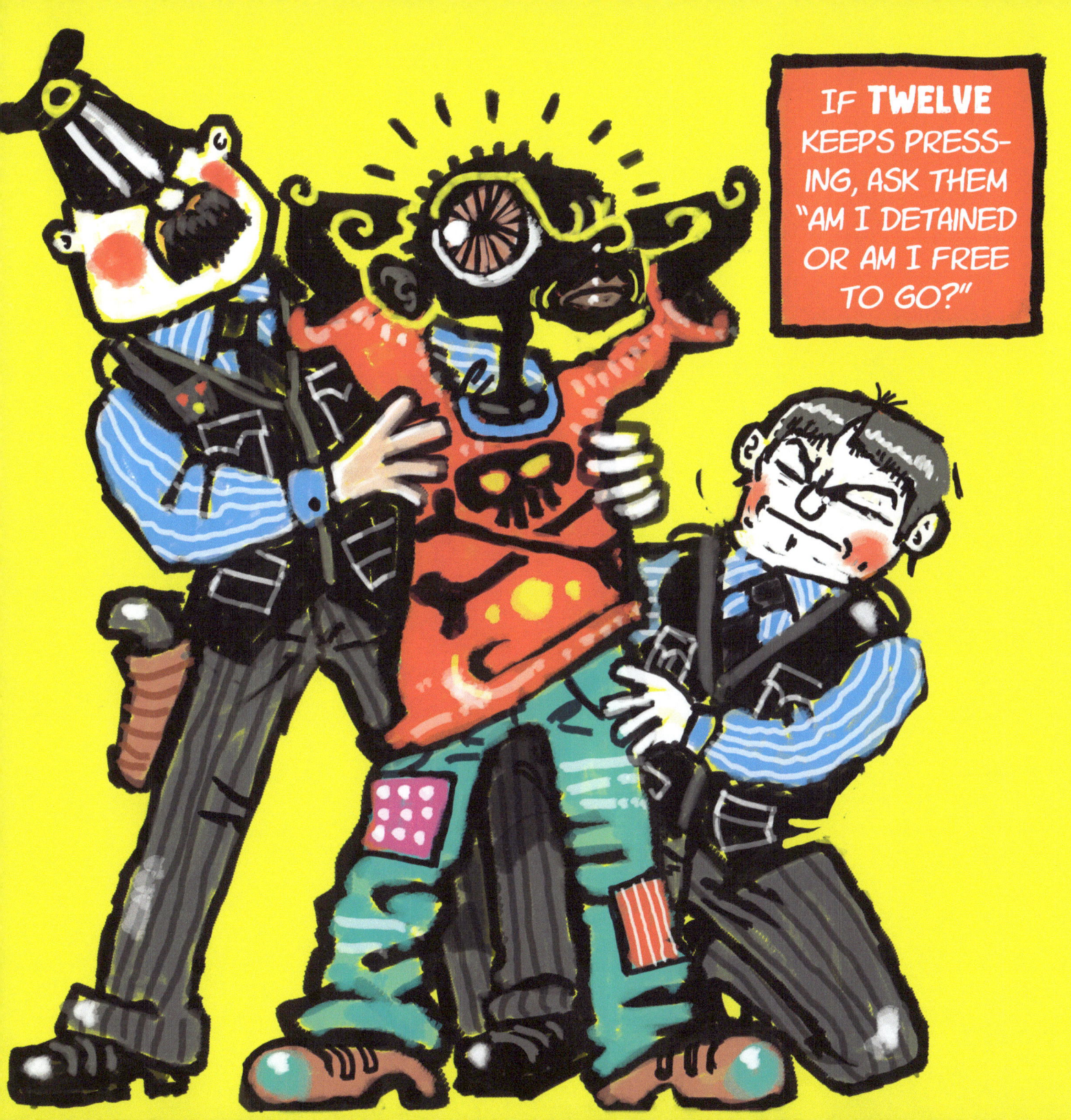

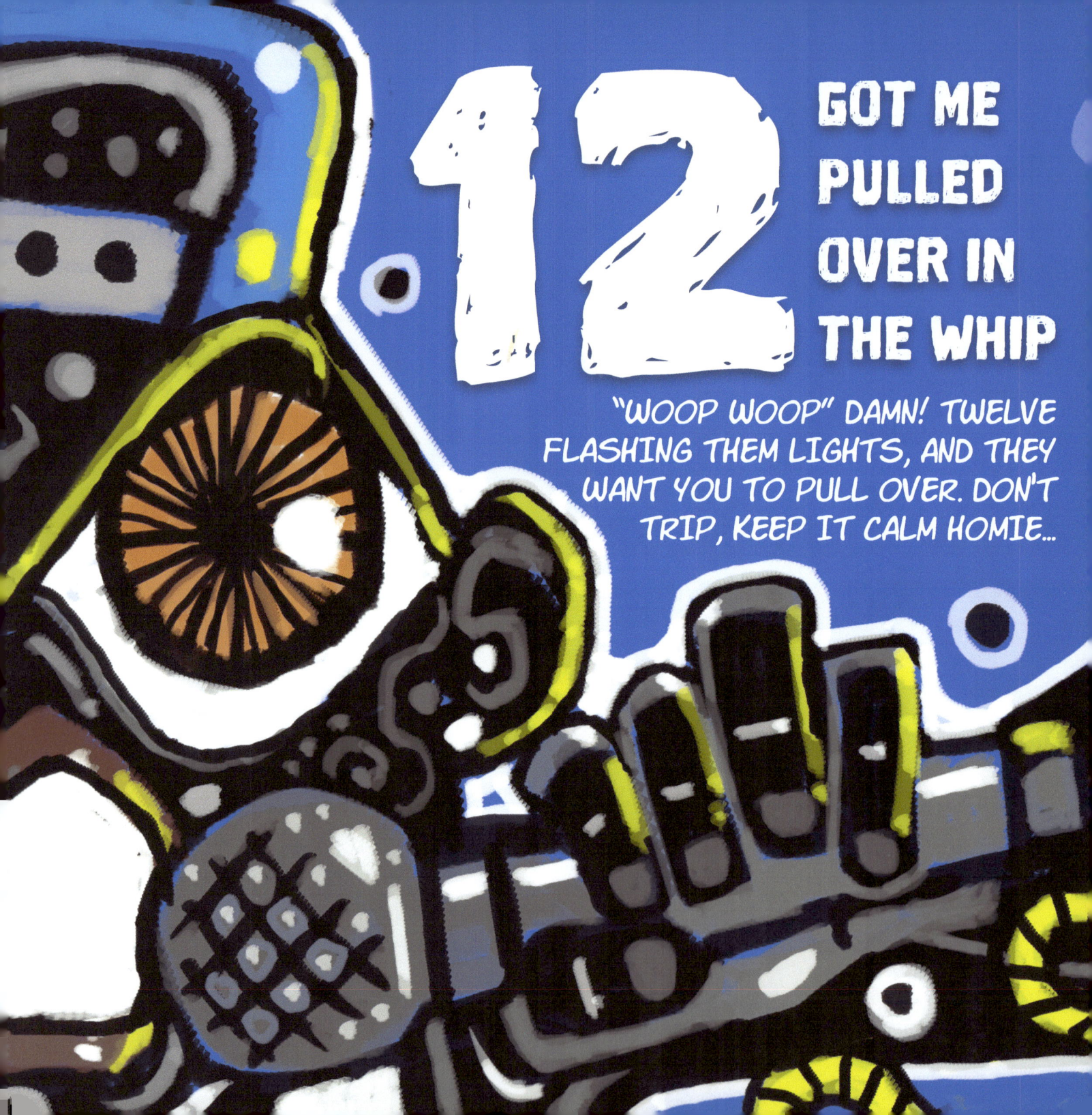

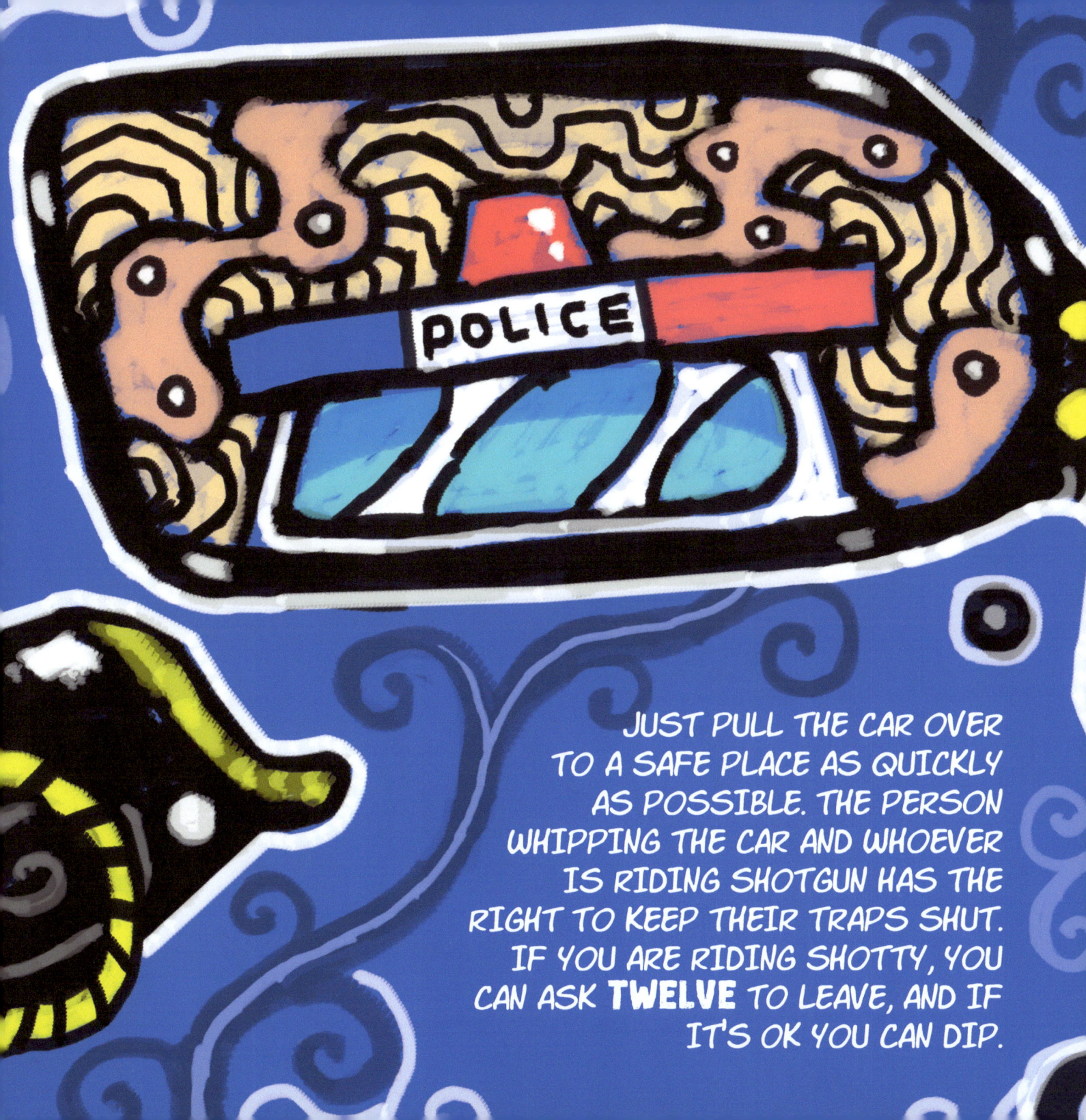

NOW THAT YOU'RE PULLED OVER AND **TWELVE** IS STILL IN THEIR CAR THE BEST THING TO DO IS ...

- TURN THE WHIP OFF.
- IF ITS AT NIGHT, TURN ON THE INTERNAL LIGHT.
- MAKE SURE TO CRACK THE WINDOW PART OF THE WAY
- THROW DEM **HANDS ON THE WHEEL**.
- IF YOU HAPPEN TO BE RIDING SHOTGUN THEN, THROW DEM **HANDS ON THE DASHBOARD**.

YOU DON'T WANT TO GIVE TWELVE ANY EXCUSE TO **REACH FOR THEIR PISTOL**. YOU WANT TO MAKE SURE THAT YOU ARE. . .

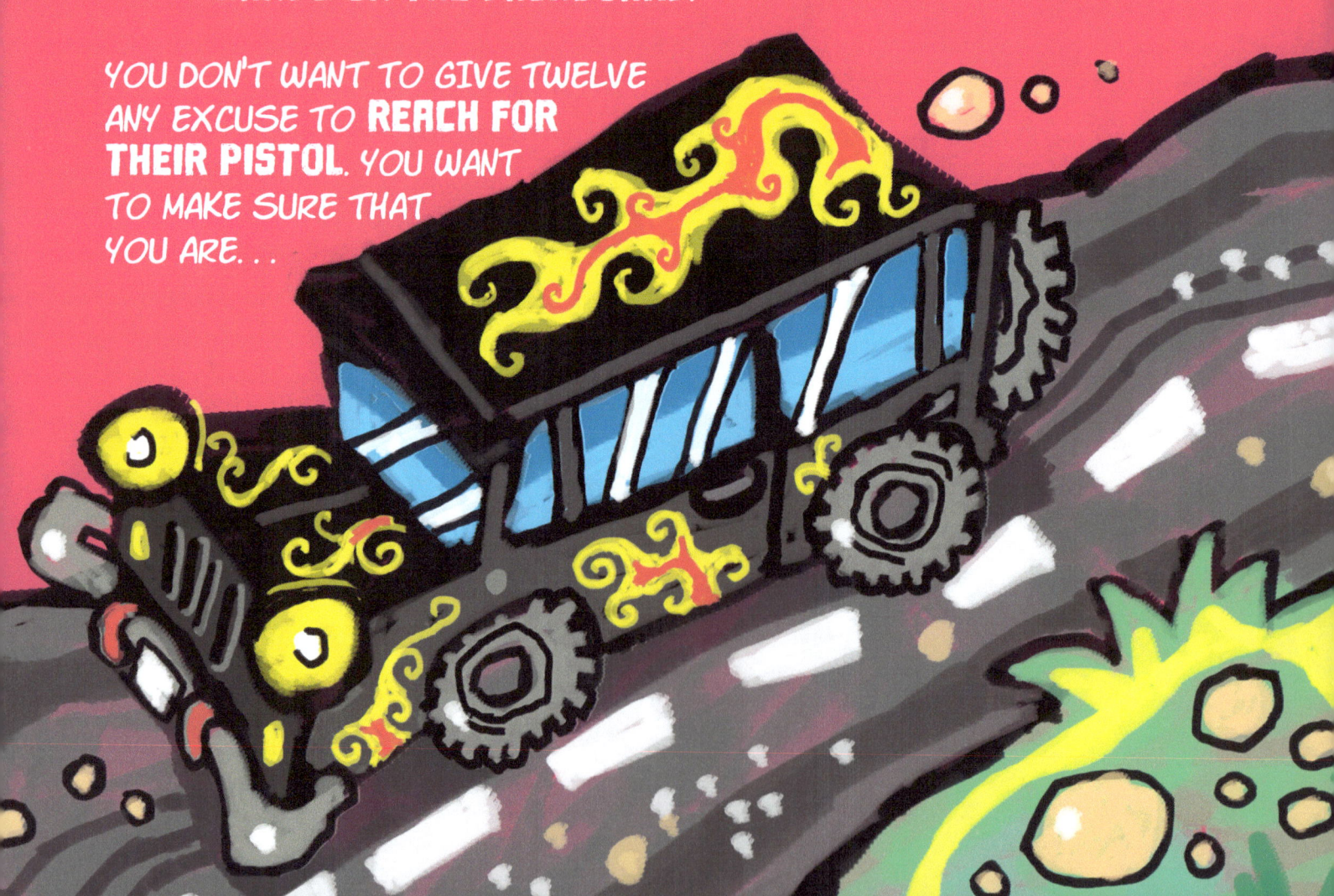

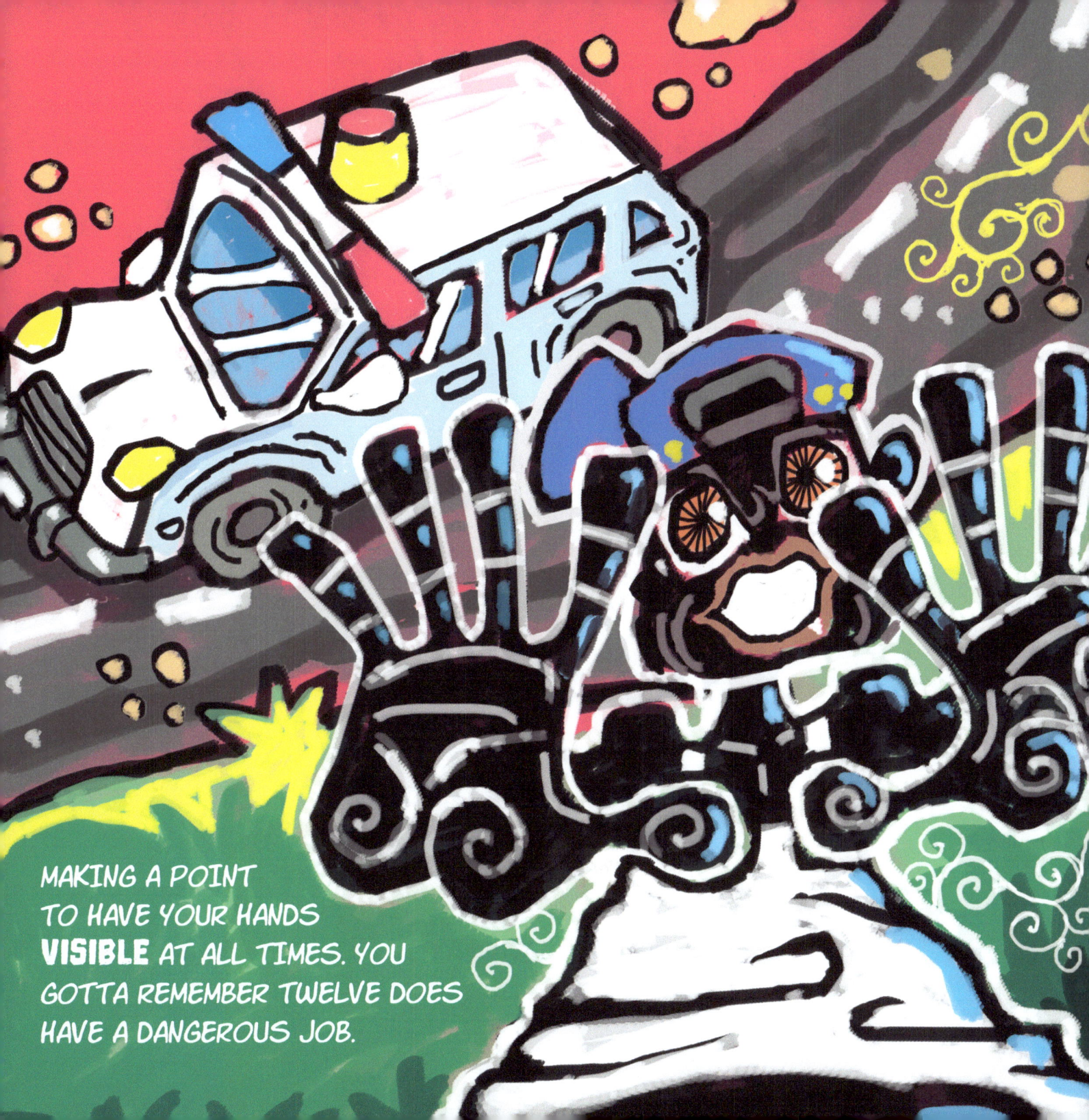

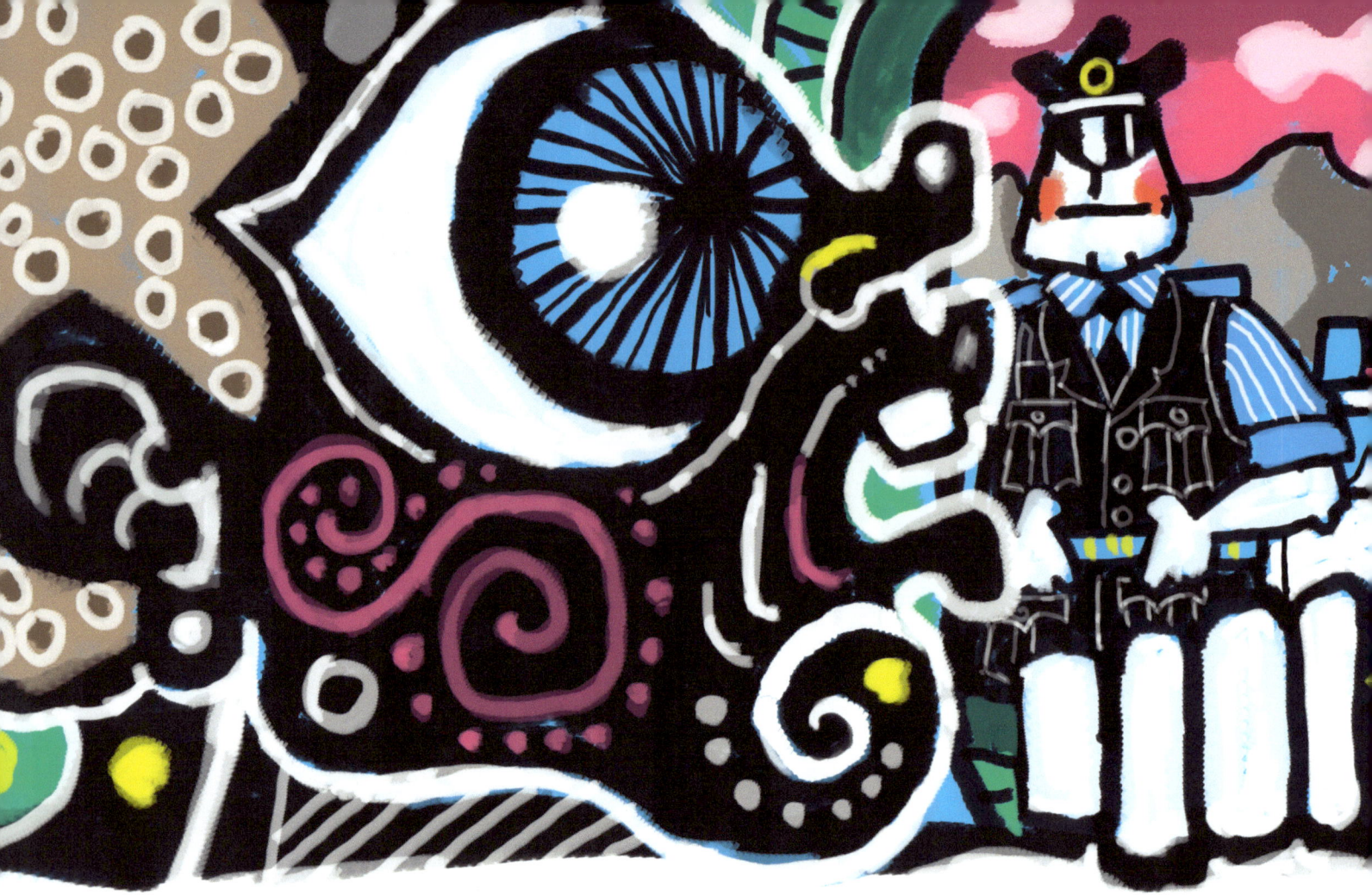

WAIT FOR TWELVE TO ASK YOU FOR YOUR DRIVERS LICENSE, REGISTRATION, AND PROOF OF INSURANCE BEFORE MAKING ANY MOVEMENTS. WHEN THEY ASK, **SHOW THEM**!

I UNDERSTAND YOU'VE SEEN VIDEOS OF TWELVE TAKING THE LAW INTO THEIR OWN HANDS. FOLLOW THE ABOVE PROCEDURES AND ATTEMPT TO MAKE THIS STOP AS SAFE AS POSSIBLE.

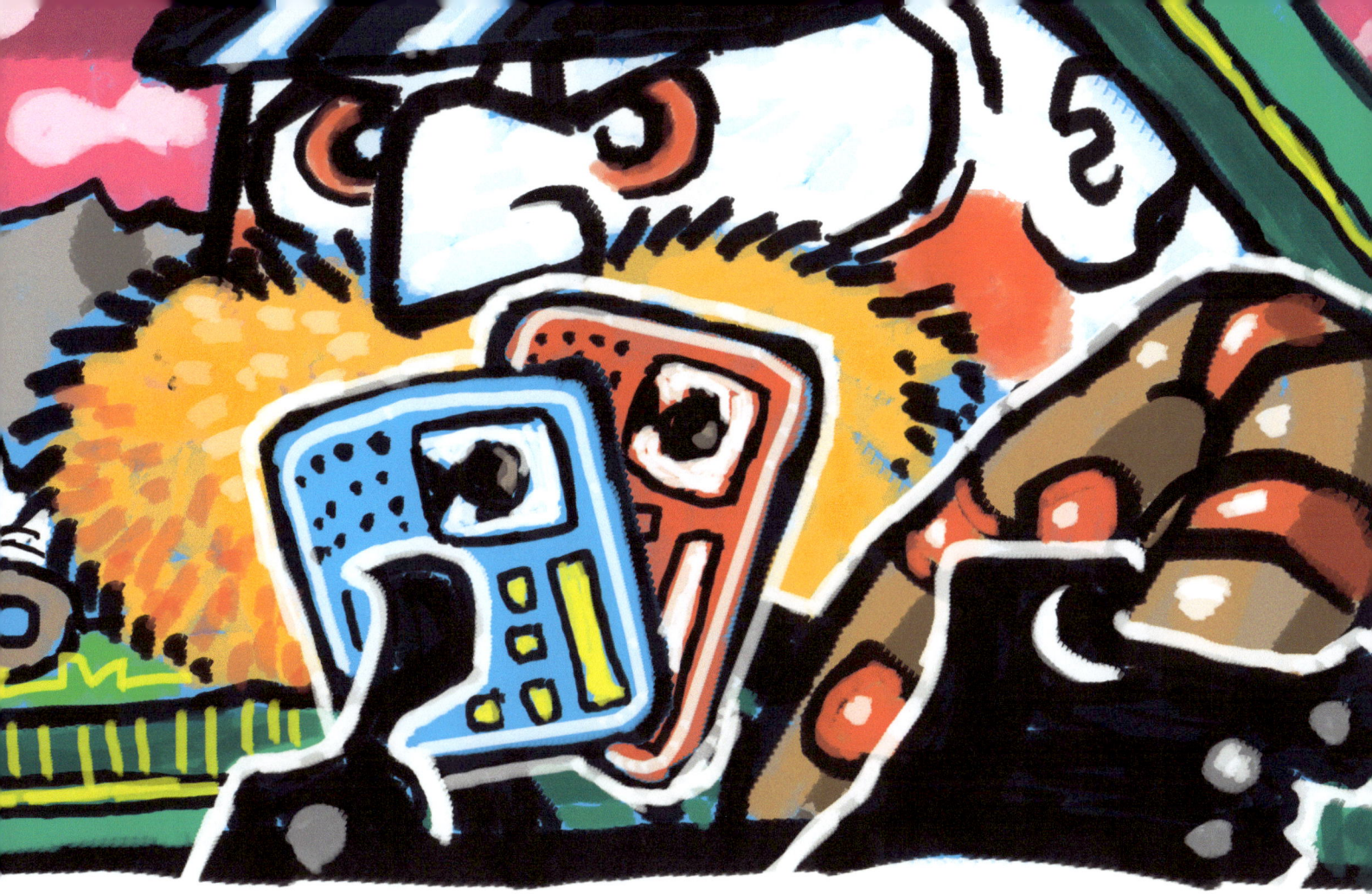

JUST BE CHILL, DON'T MAKE ANY SKETCHY OR QUICK MOVEMENTS; **AKA DON'T MOVE!** IF TWELVE TRIES TO GO HARD AND SEARCH YOUR WHIP, YOU HAVE THE RIGHT TO TELL THEM YOU **DO NOT CONSENT** TO A SEARCH.

THEY COULD TRY TO GET IN YOUR HEAD LIKE THEY 'BOUT TO BRING THE DOGS THROUGH. THESE ARE ALL TACTICS, JUST CALMLY ASK "AM I BEING DETAINED, OR AM I FREE TO GO?"

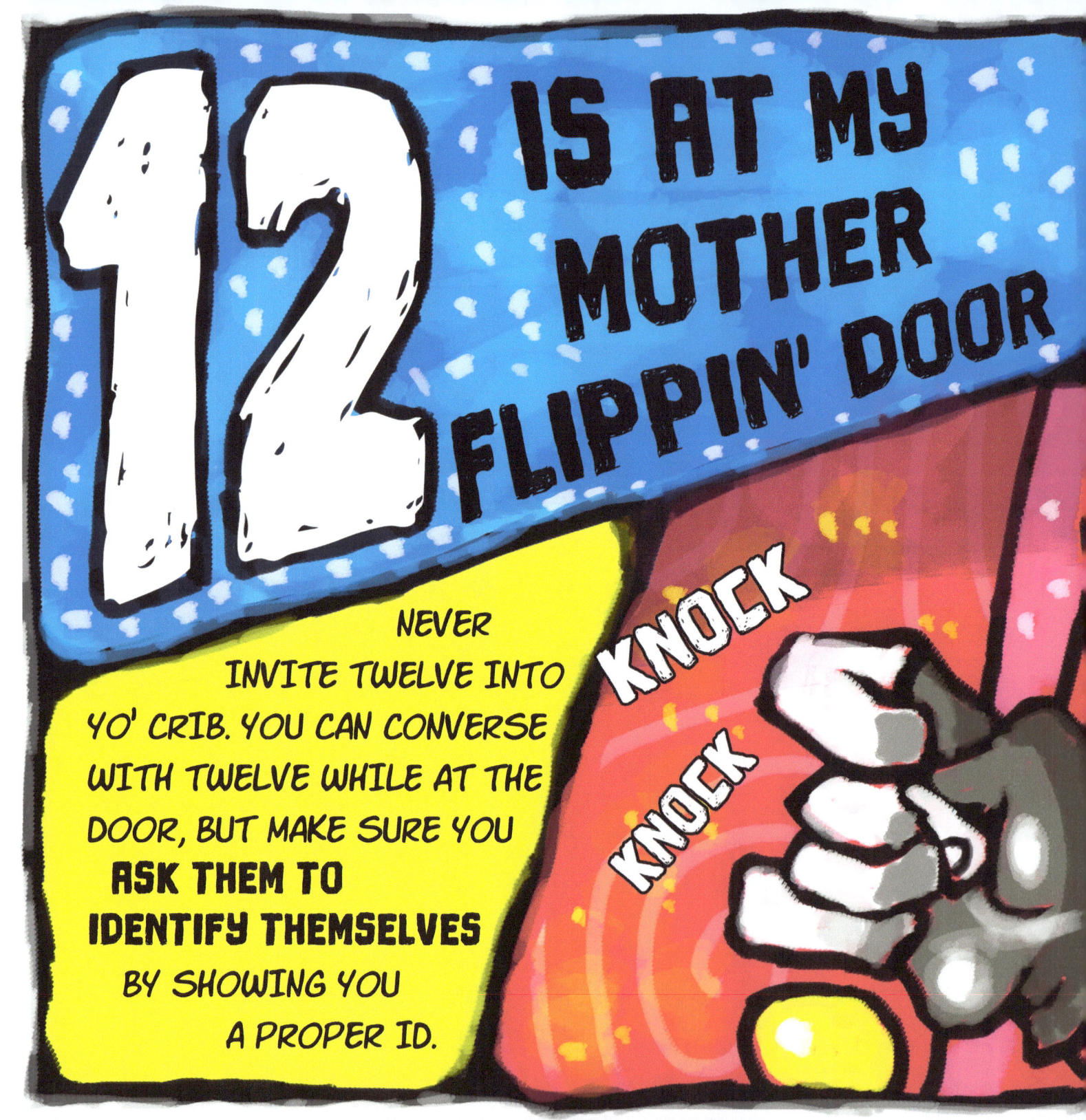

THE ONLY WAY YOU ARE REQUIRED TO LET TWELVE IN IS IF THEY HAVE A **WARRANT**. THE GOOD OLD 4TH AMENDMENT GOT YOUR BACK. IF NONE OF THOSE THINGS ARE PROVIDED, THEN KEEP YOUR DISTANCE AND TELL THEM TO HAVE A NICE DAY. THEY HAVE NO LEGAL RIGHT TO ARREST OR BE IN THE CRIB.

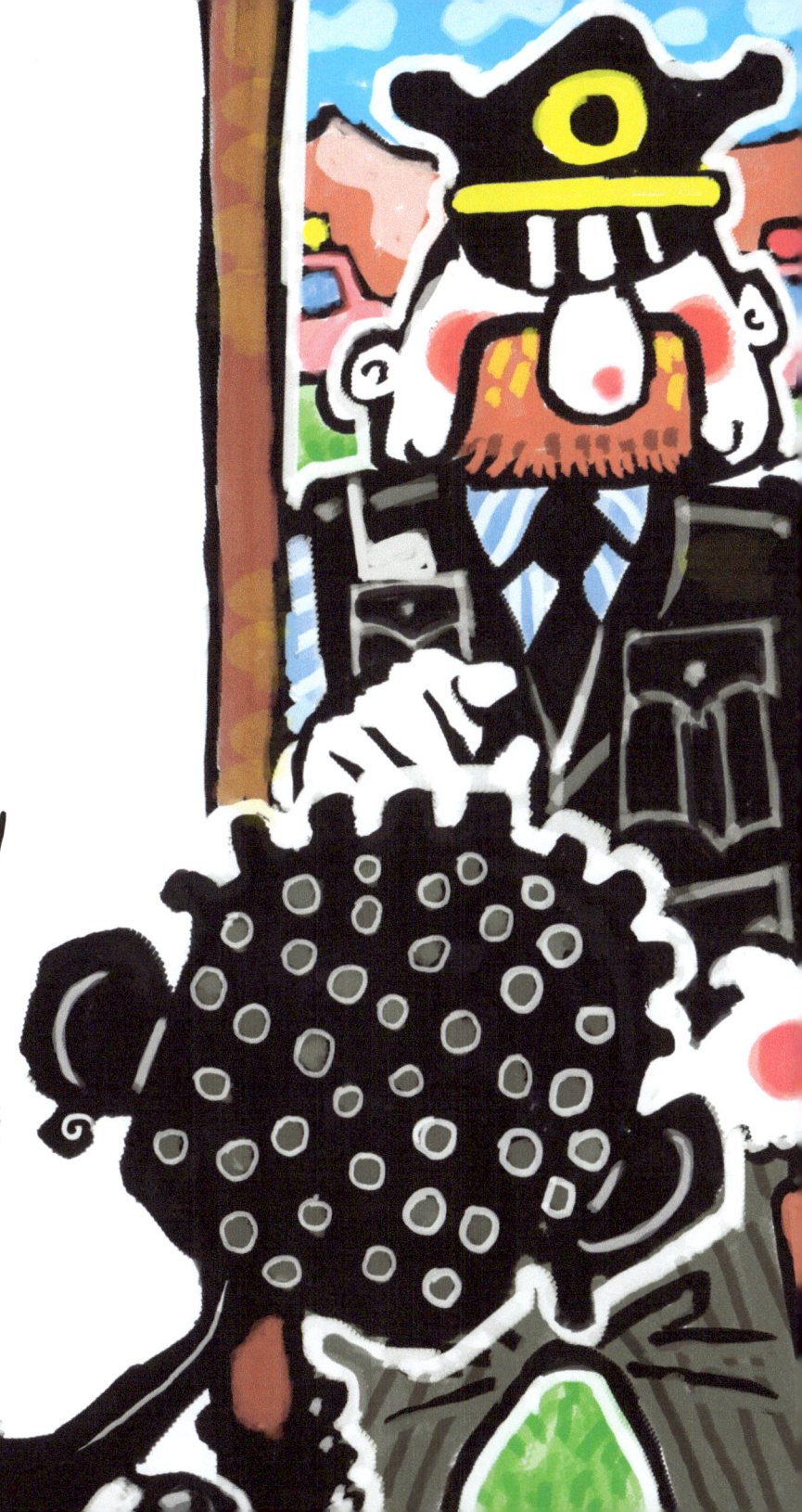

IF TWELVE DOES HAVE THE WARRANT, TELL THEM TO SLIDE IT UNDER THE DOOR OR HAVE IT SO YOU CAN READ IT TO MAKE SURE IT'S LEGIT. IF YOU HAVEN'T SEEN THE MOVIE 'TRAINING DAY,' THERE IS A SCENE WHERE THE COPS USE A CHINESE FOOD MENU TO ILLEGALLY SEARCH. **CRAZY RIGHT**?! SO MAKE SURE YOU **READ** THAT PAPER!!!!

THE PURPOSE OF A SEARCH WARRANT IS THAT IT ALLOWS TWELVE TO ENTER THE ADDRESS LISTED. BUT DON'T GET IT TWISTED, THEY CAN'T GO EVERYWHERE IN YOUR CRIB. THEY ARE ONLY ALLOWED TO SEARCH FOR **WHAT** IS LISTED ON THE WARRANT, AND THE **AREAS** LISTED!

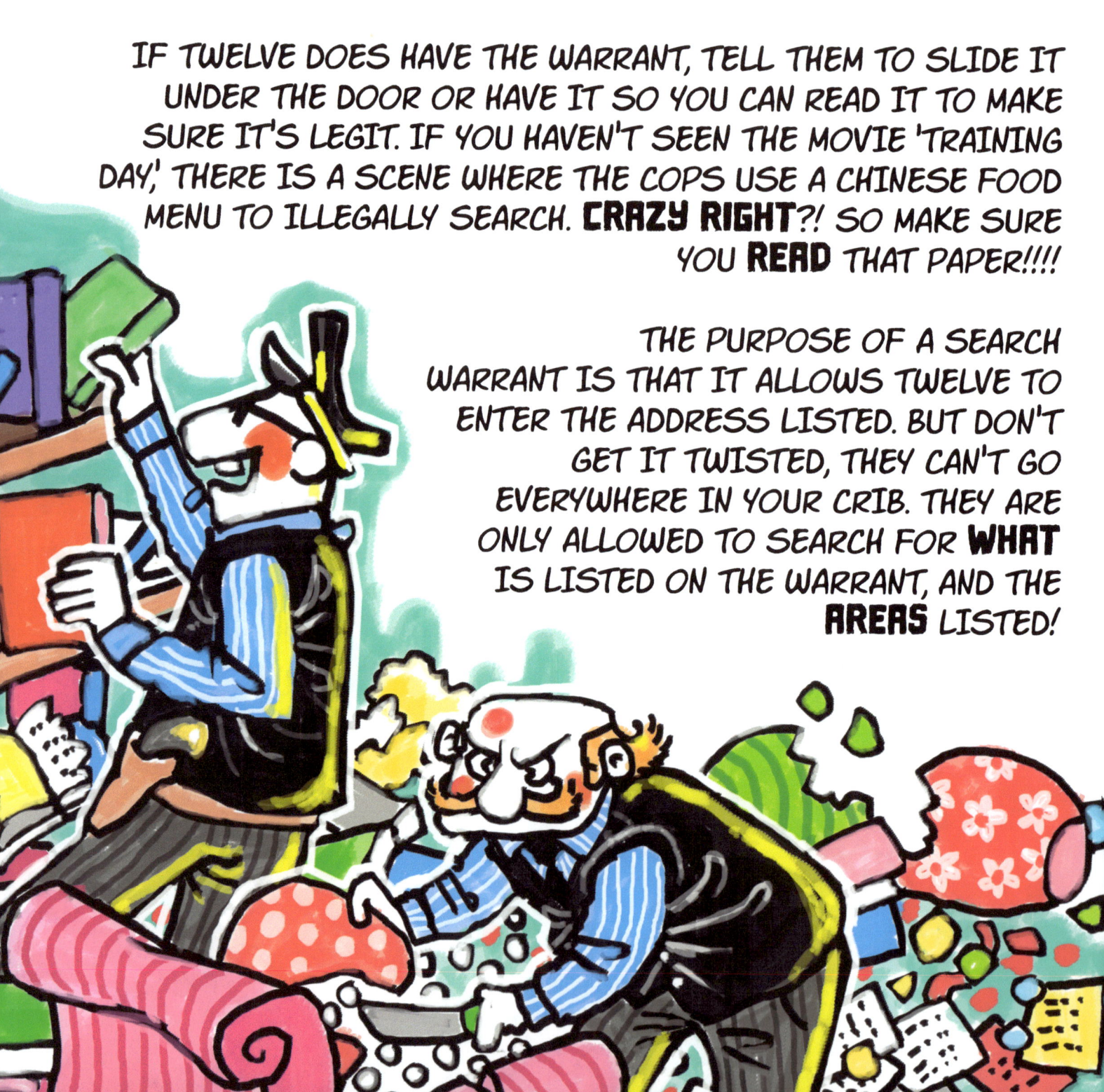

EVEN IF TWELVE GOT THAT MAGIC TICKET, YOU STILL HAVE RIGHTS. SO MAKE SURE TO **KEEP THAT A$$ SILENT**.

WHILE THEY SEARCH, KEEP IT QUIET, WATCH WHAT THEY DO, WHERE THEY'RE SEARCHING, AND WHAT THEY TAKE!

SO WHAT HAPPENS IF YOU CHILLIN AT THE HOMIES SPOT AND **TWELVE** COMES THROUGH?! LET TWELVE KNOW YOU ARE JUST A GUEST AT THE CRIB AND YOU DON'T HAVE THE AUTHORITY TO LET THEM INSIDE WITHOUT THE HOMEOWNERS PERMISSION.

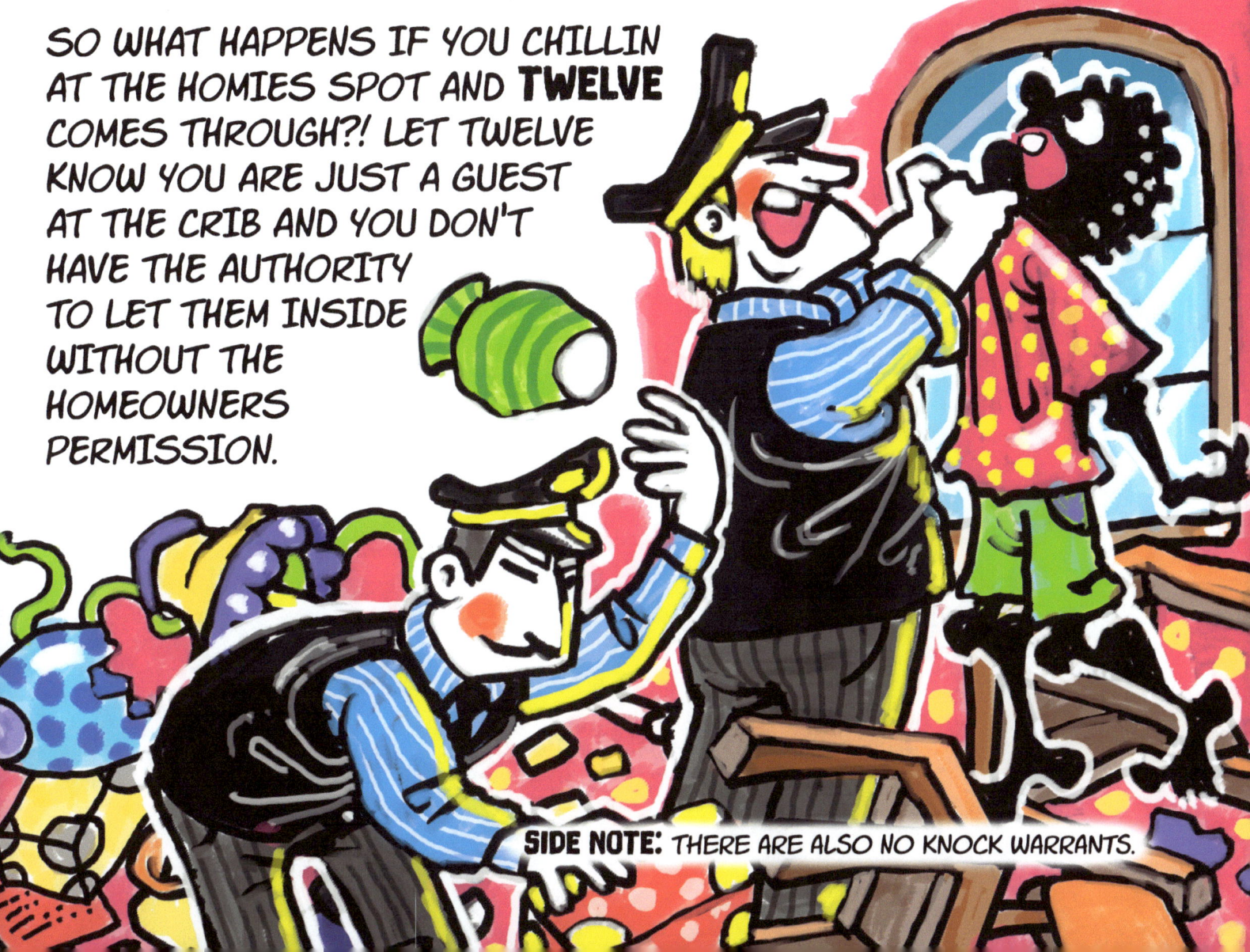

SIDE NOTE: THERE ARE ALSO NO KNOCK WARRANTS.

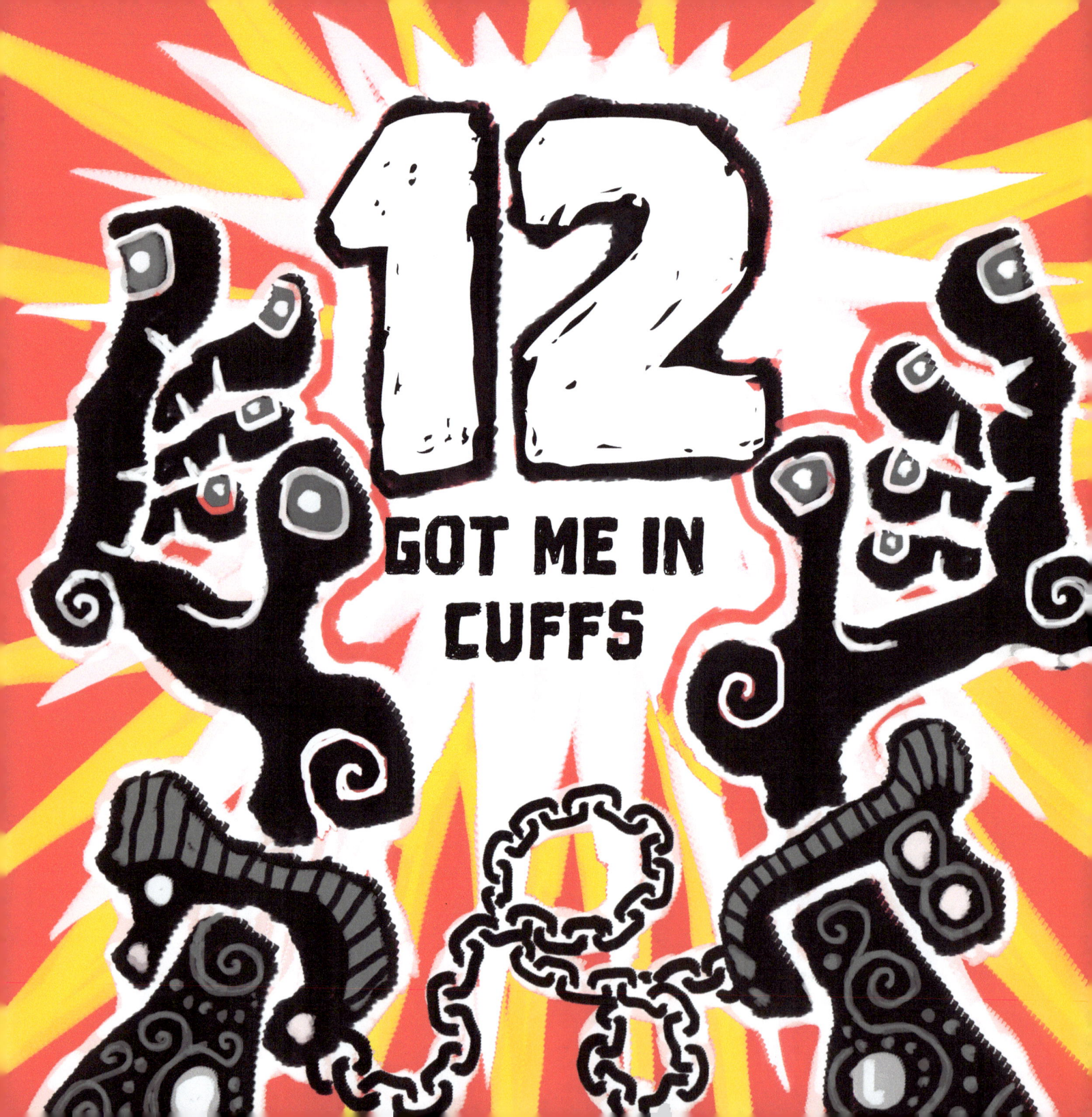

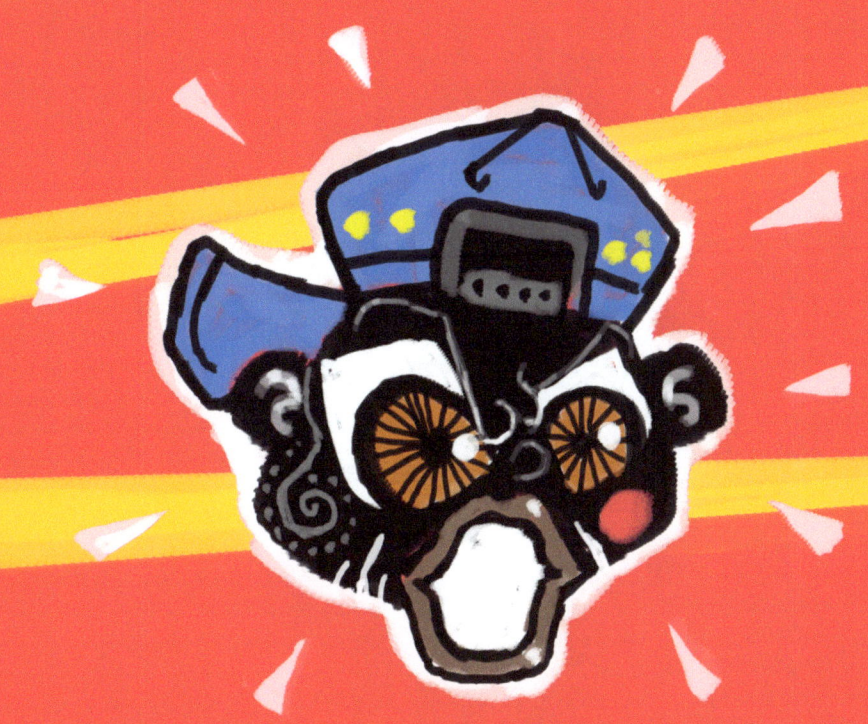

IF YOU CUFFED UP BY **TWELVE** AND YOUR FUNDS ARE LOW, YOU DO HAVE THE RIGHT TO GET A P.D. AKA **PUBLIC DEFENDER**. DON'T SAY SH*T, SIGN SH*T, OR DO ANYTHING 'TIL YOUR LAWYER ARRIVES.

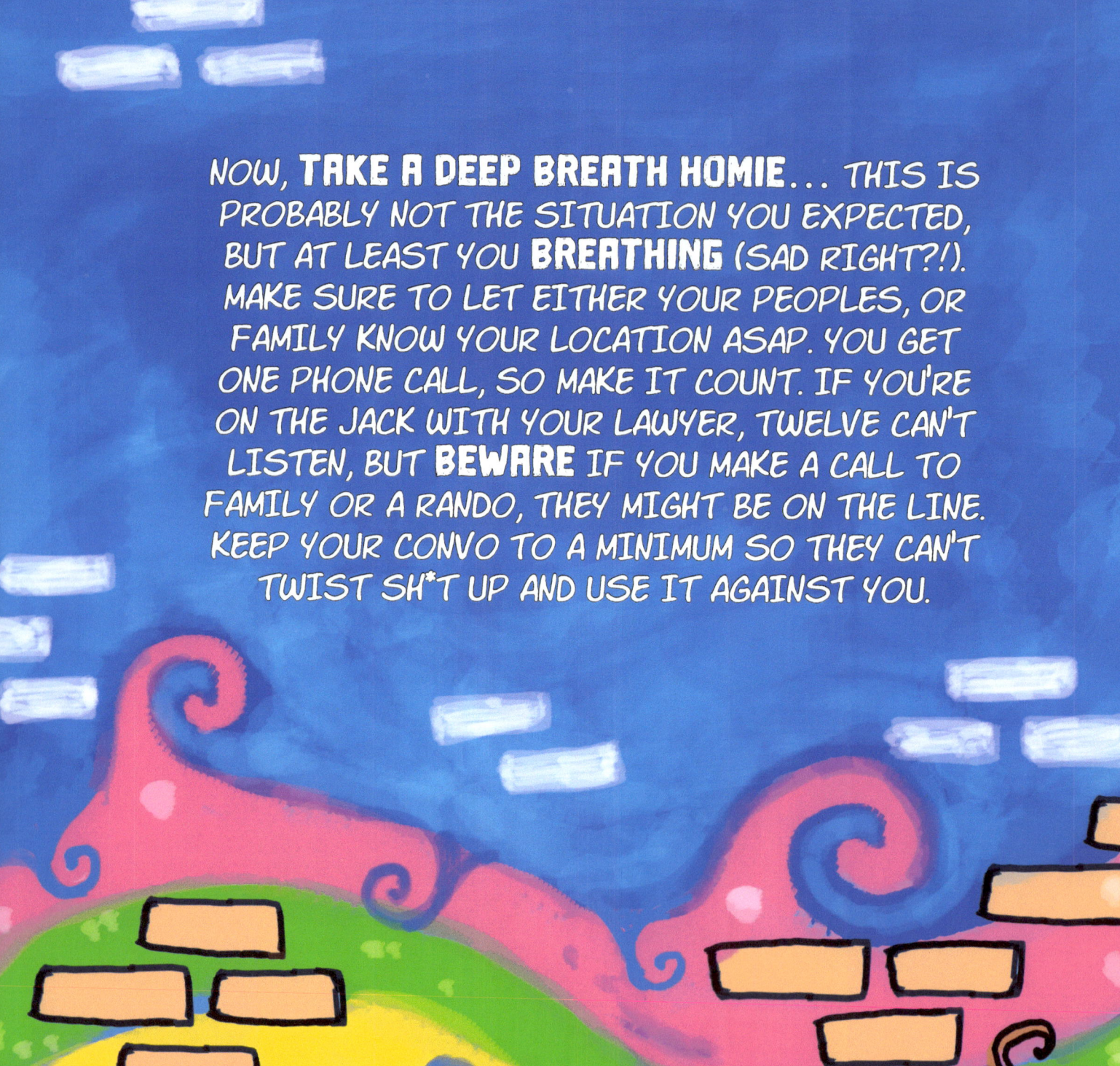

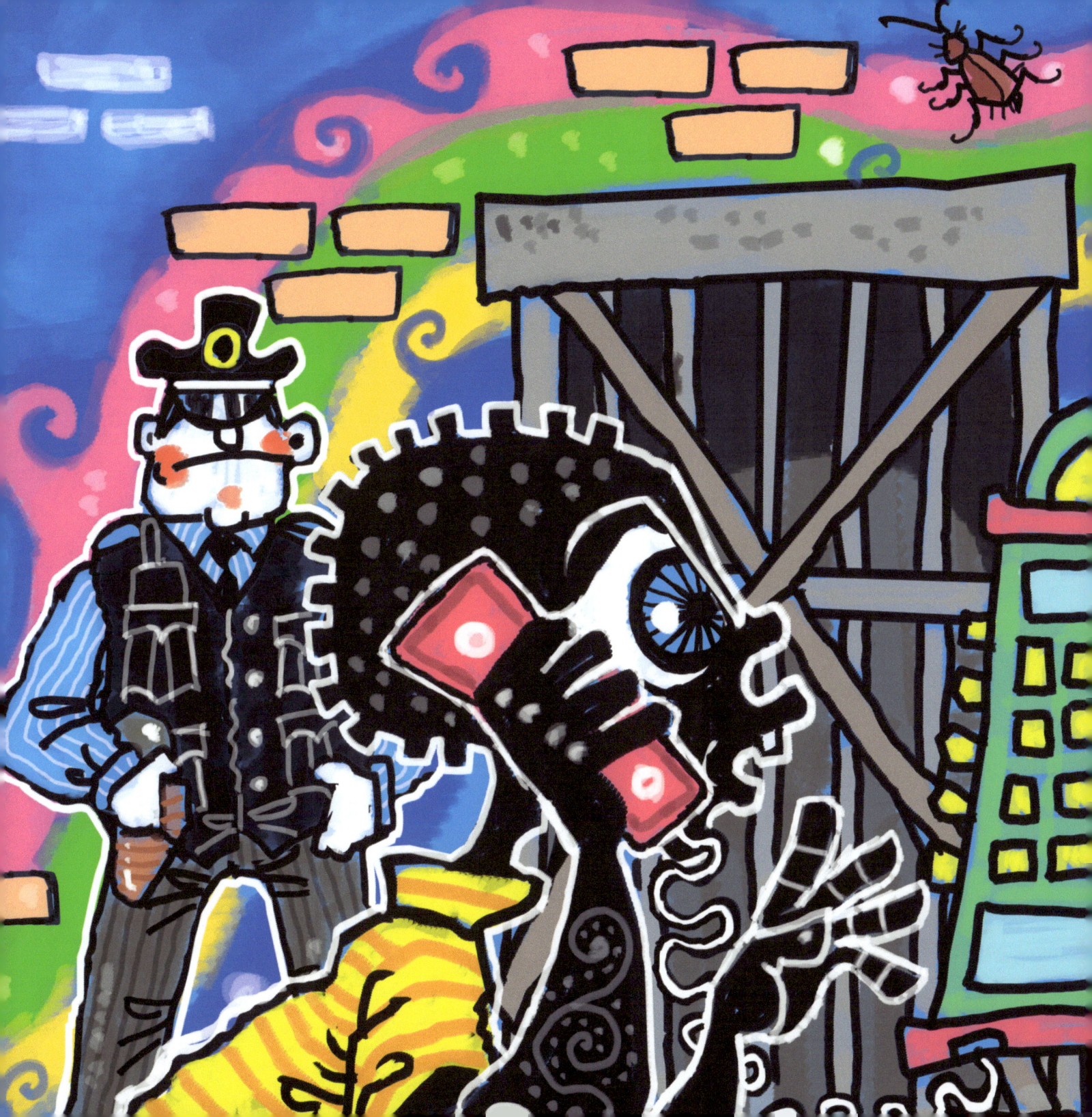

12 VIOLATED MY RIGHTS

IF YOU FEEL LIKE TWELVE VIOLATED YOU IN ANY WAY, SHAPE, OR FORM...

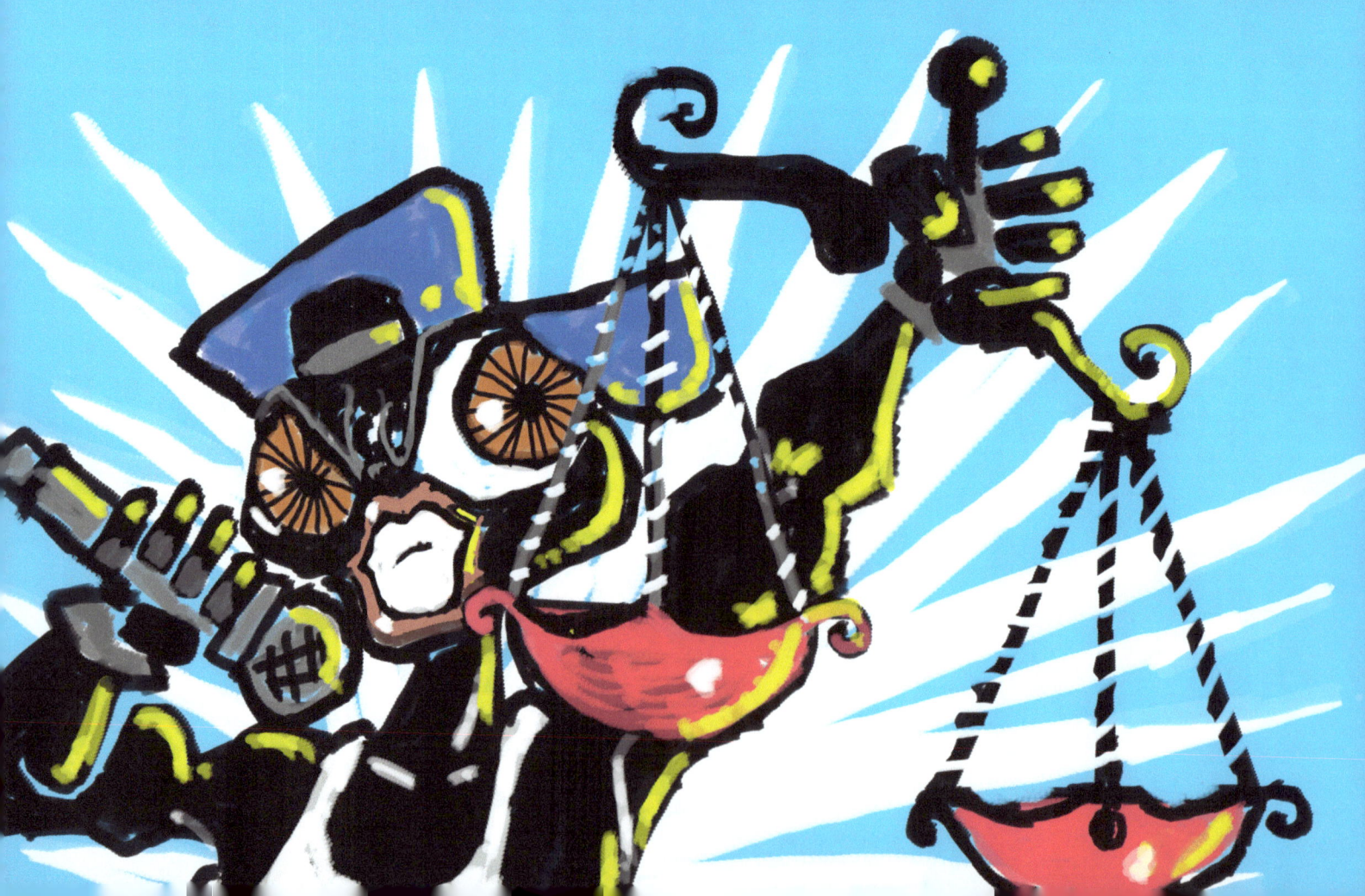

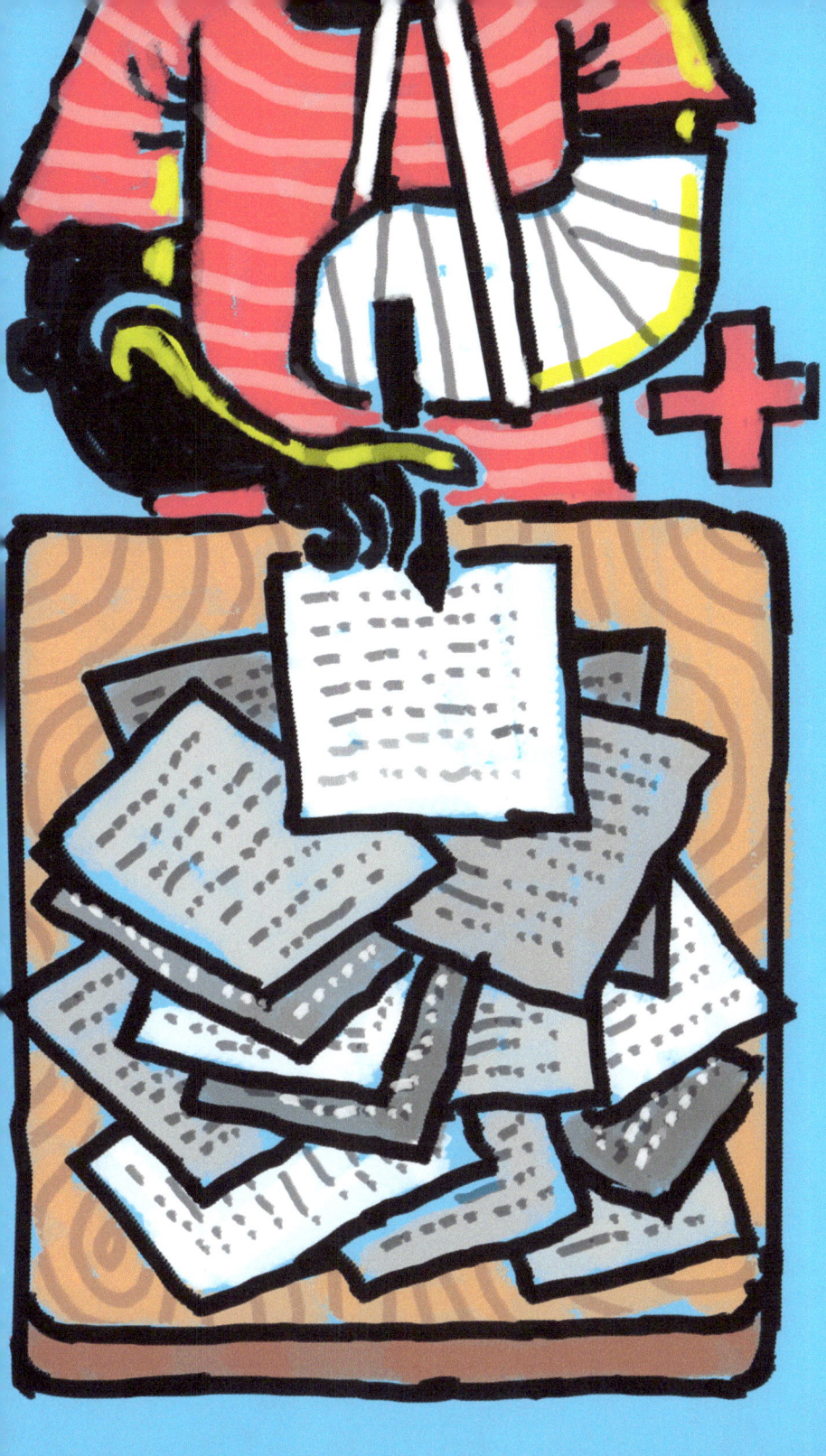

THIS IS WHAT YOU GOTTA DO:

- WRITE DOWN THE BADGE NUMBER AND TWELVE'S NAME.

- GET CONTACT INFO IF THERE HAPPENS TO BE A WITNESS.

- IF YOU GOT HURT, YOU NEED TO GO AND SEEK MEDICAL ATTENTION ASAP! TAKE PICTURES OF THE INJURIES, AND SAVE ALL THAT PAPERWORK.

- FILE A COMPLAINT WITH INTERNAL AFFAIRS (YOU CAN DO THAT ANONYMOUSLY) IF NEED BE.

I KNOW THIS MAY SEEM LIKE A LOT OF WORK BUT IT'S AGAINST THE LAW FOR TWELVE TO ACT THIS WAY. DO YOUR DUE DILIGENCE, **THIS COULD SAVE THE NEXT HOMIES LIFE.**

F12

WHEN IT COMES TO ABUSE AND BRUTALITY

Unfortunately, today's reality could place you as a witness to **TWELVE** acting up... I hope this never happens to you. If this does, this would be the safest way to get involved:

Get your phone out and start **RECORDING**! Keep a safe distance tho, you don't wanna obstruct or interfere with the ongoing situation. You always got the right to observe and record events that happen in public, so you're good! Let it be known you got your phone out, and that you are recording. The point of being vocal about the recording is so that you don't get into trouble. Let's just say for some reason a person can't be recorded (they have a reasonable expectation of privacy). At least you have it on record; you the recorder have made it known. Always protect **YOURSELF**!

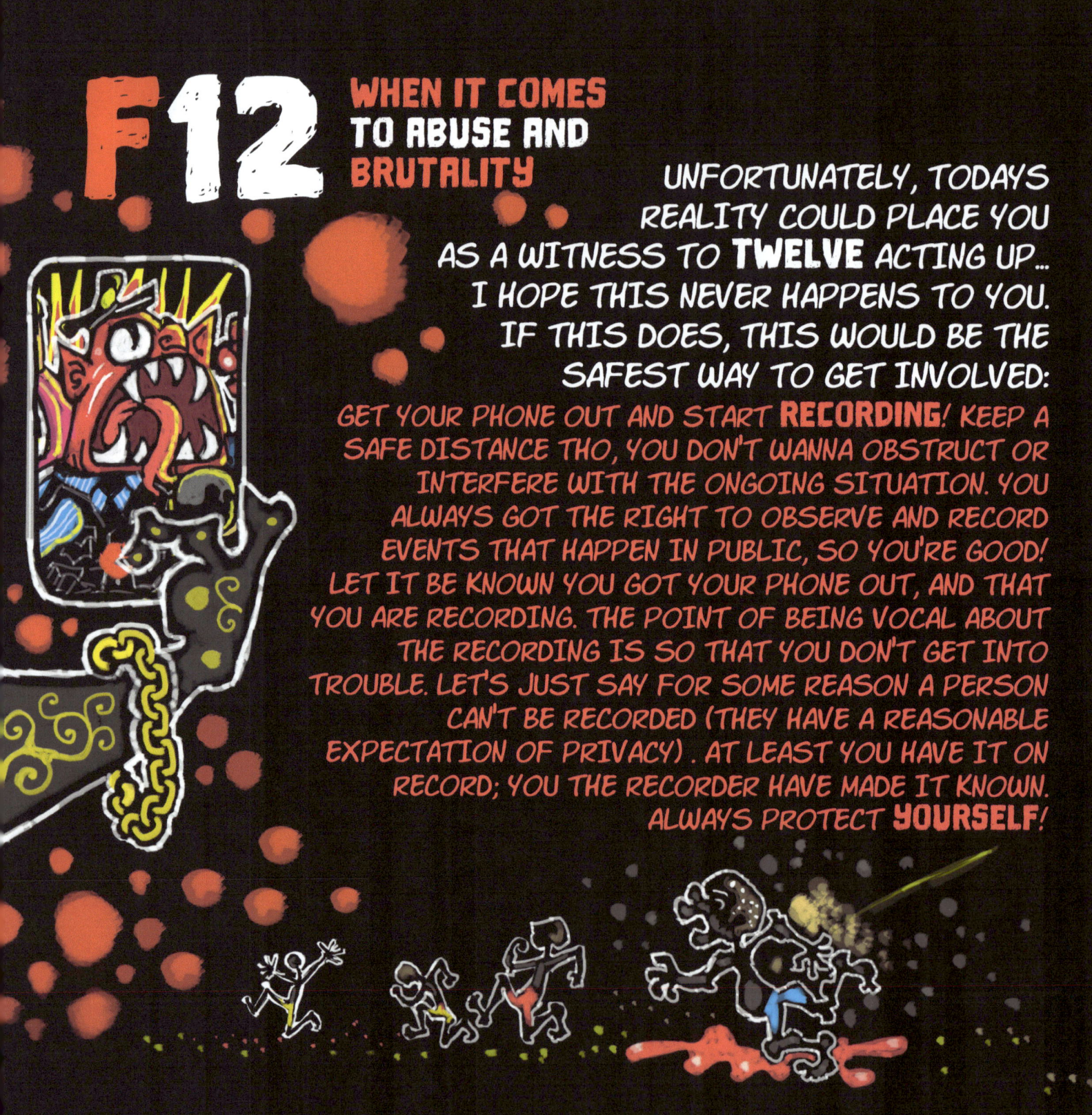

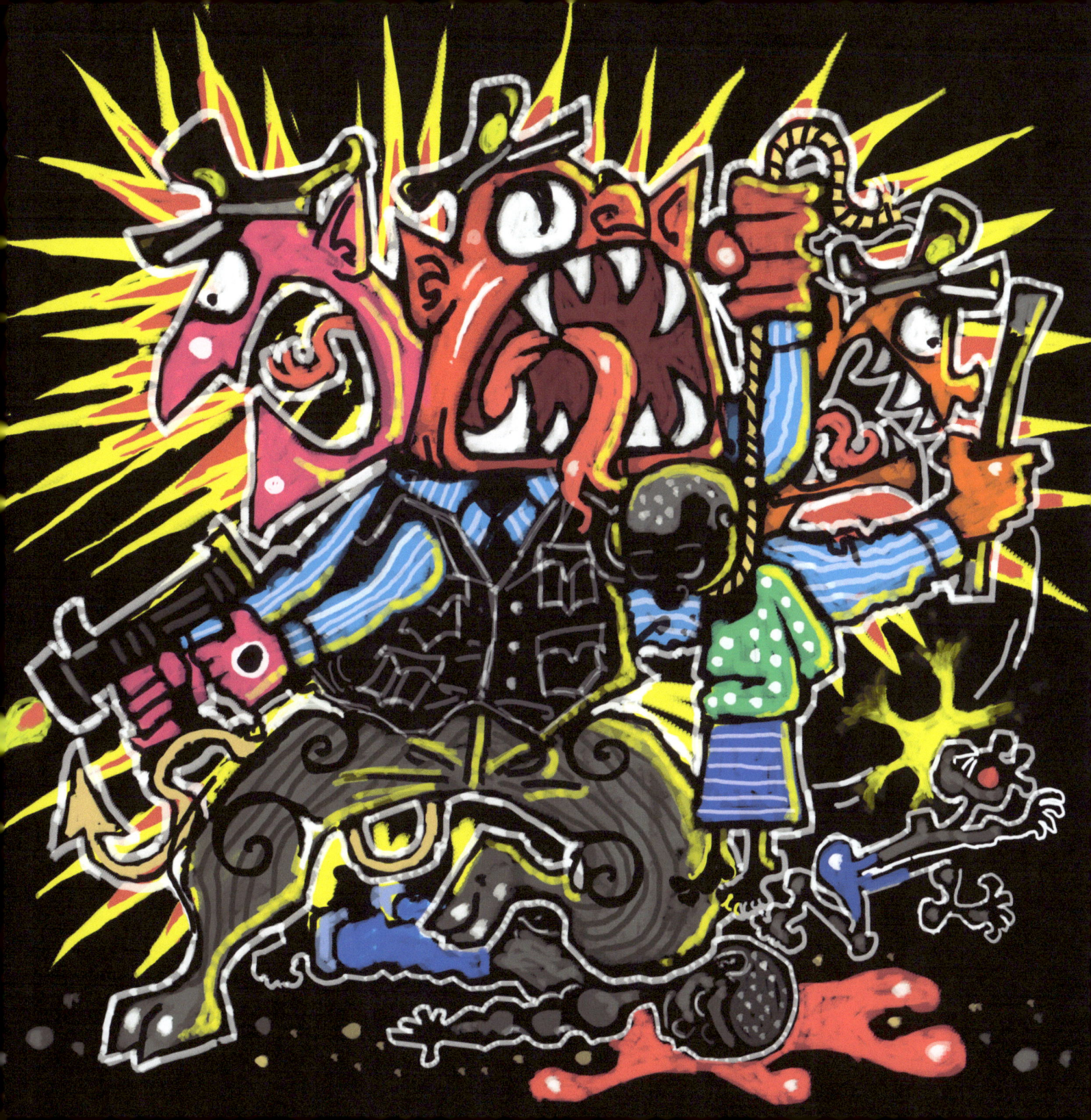

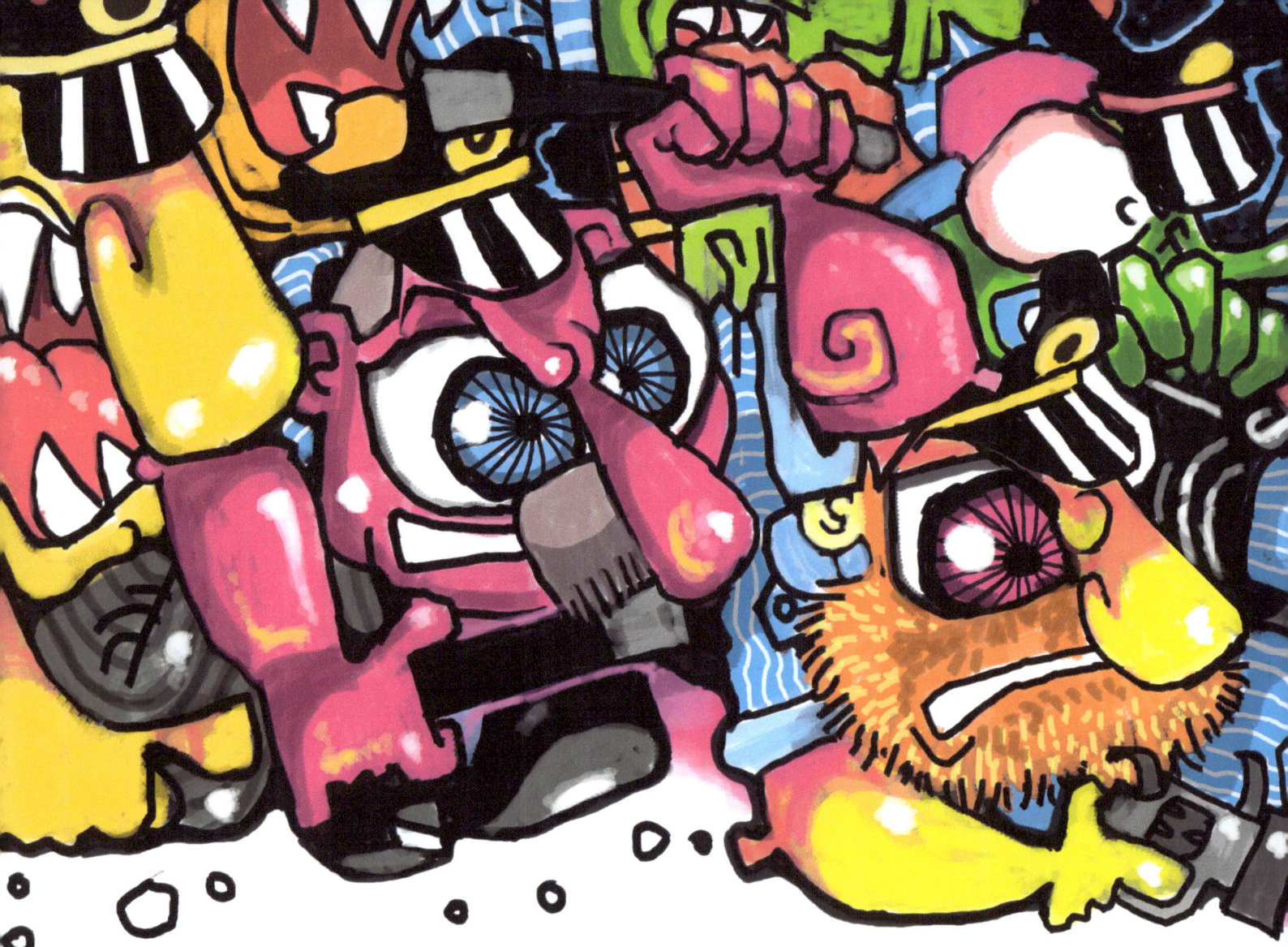

NEVER LET TWELVE TAKE YOUR PHONE AWAY OR DEMAND TO SEE PICTURES OR VIDEO; THEY LAWFULLY CANNOT. IF TWELVE ORDERS YOU TO STOP WHAT YOU'RE DOING YOU GOTTA STAY YOUR CALMEST, USE A FIRM TONE AND SAY:
"I AM WITHIN MY RIGHTS! I CAN RECORD THIS IN PLAIN VIEW."
UNDER THE FIRST AMENDMENT, YOU CAN DO THIS.

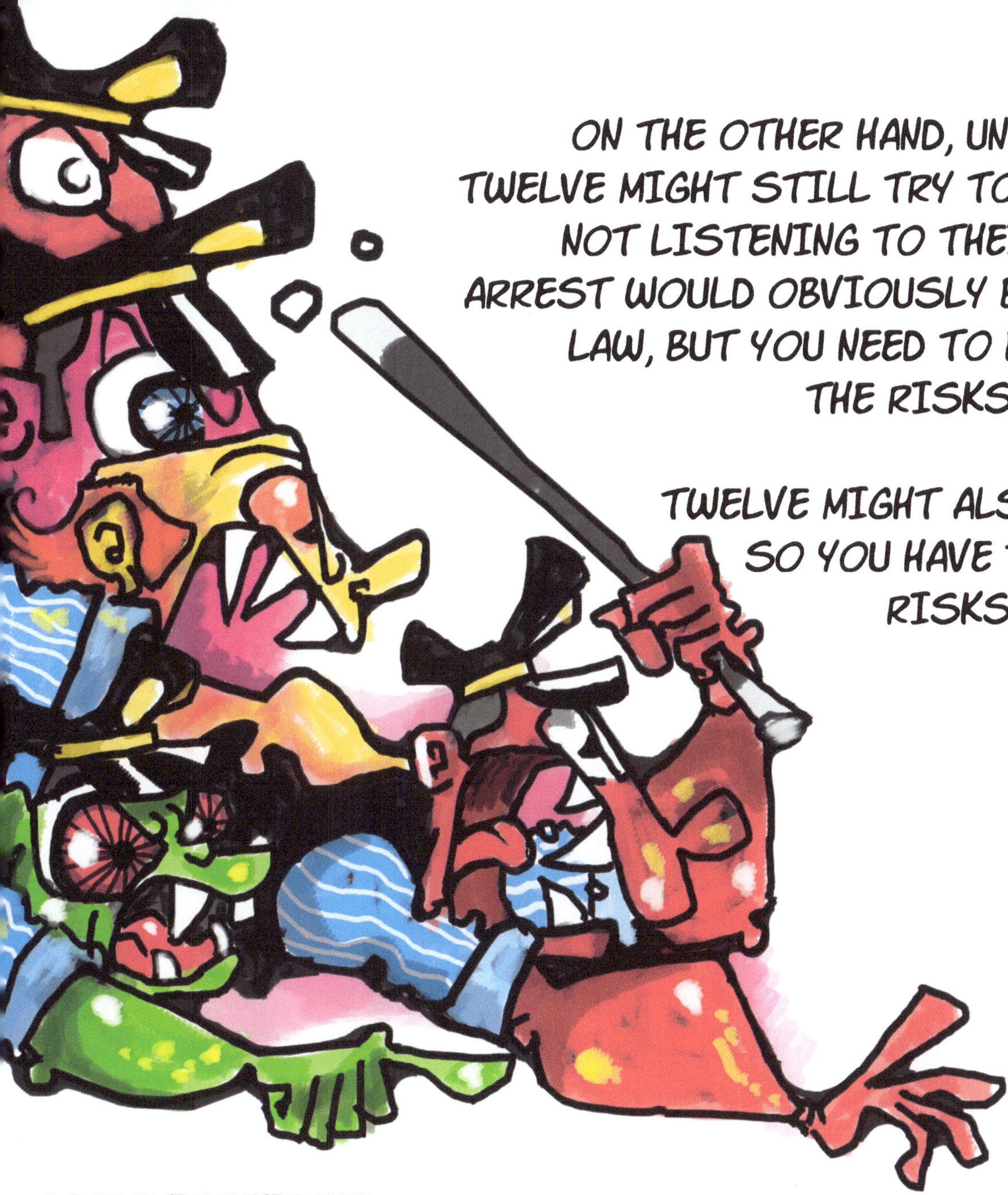

ON THE OTHER HAND, UNDERSTAND THAT TWELVE MIGHT STILL TRY TO CUFF YOU FOR NOT LISTENING TO THEIR ORDERS. THE ARREST WOULD OBVIOUSLY BE AGAINST THE LAW, BUT YOU NEED TO FIGURE OUT IF THE RISKS ARE WORTH IT.

TWELVE MIGHT ALSO SEARCH YOU, SO YOU HAVE TO TAKE THOSE RISKS INTO ACCOUNT. WOULD I STILL RECORD?

... HELL YEAH!

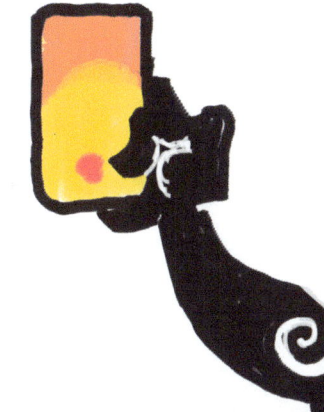

WHILE RECORDING, MAKE SURE TO GET ANY USEFUL INFO LIKE BADGE NUMBER, NAME OR PATROL UNIT. MAKE SURE TO STATE THE USE OF ANY WEAPONS, OR ILLEGAL HOLDS YOU SEE.

TIPS TO KEEP YOU SAFE

Whenever around Twelve try to remain calm, even if you are in a situation that wasn't your fault. Be smart, try n use the law to your advantage. I mean Twelve would, right?

...I know it isn't right or lawful to be harassed by the same people who are supposed to protect you. The best way to stay alive on these skreets is to comply to the best of your abilities. So don't run, don't resist, and don't get in the way of Twelve!

YOUR LIFE DEPENDS ON IT.

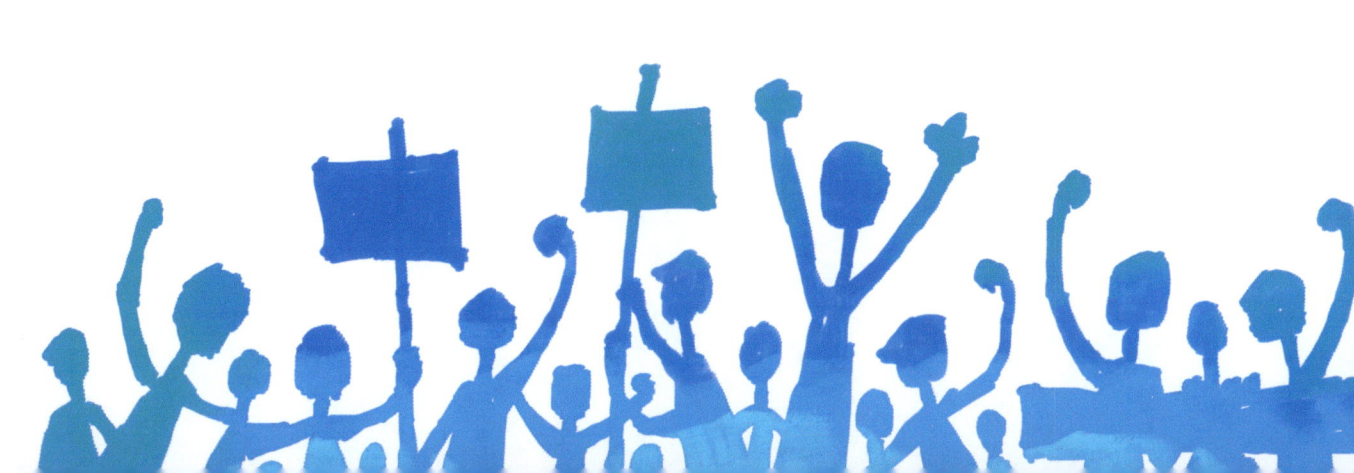

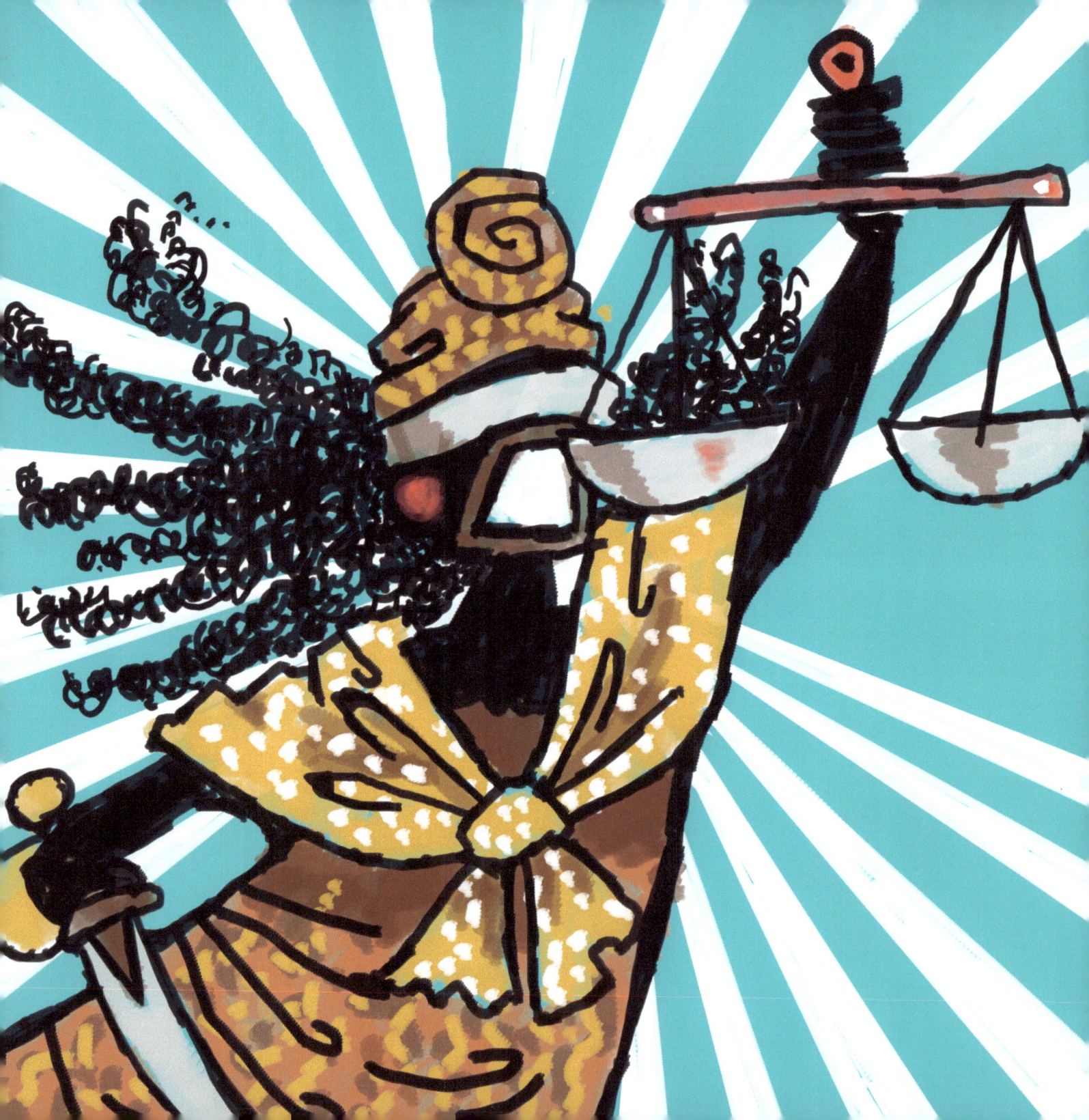

JUSTICE FOR THE HOMIES

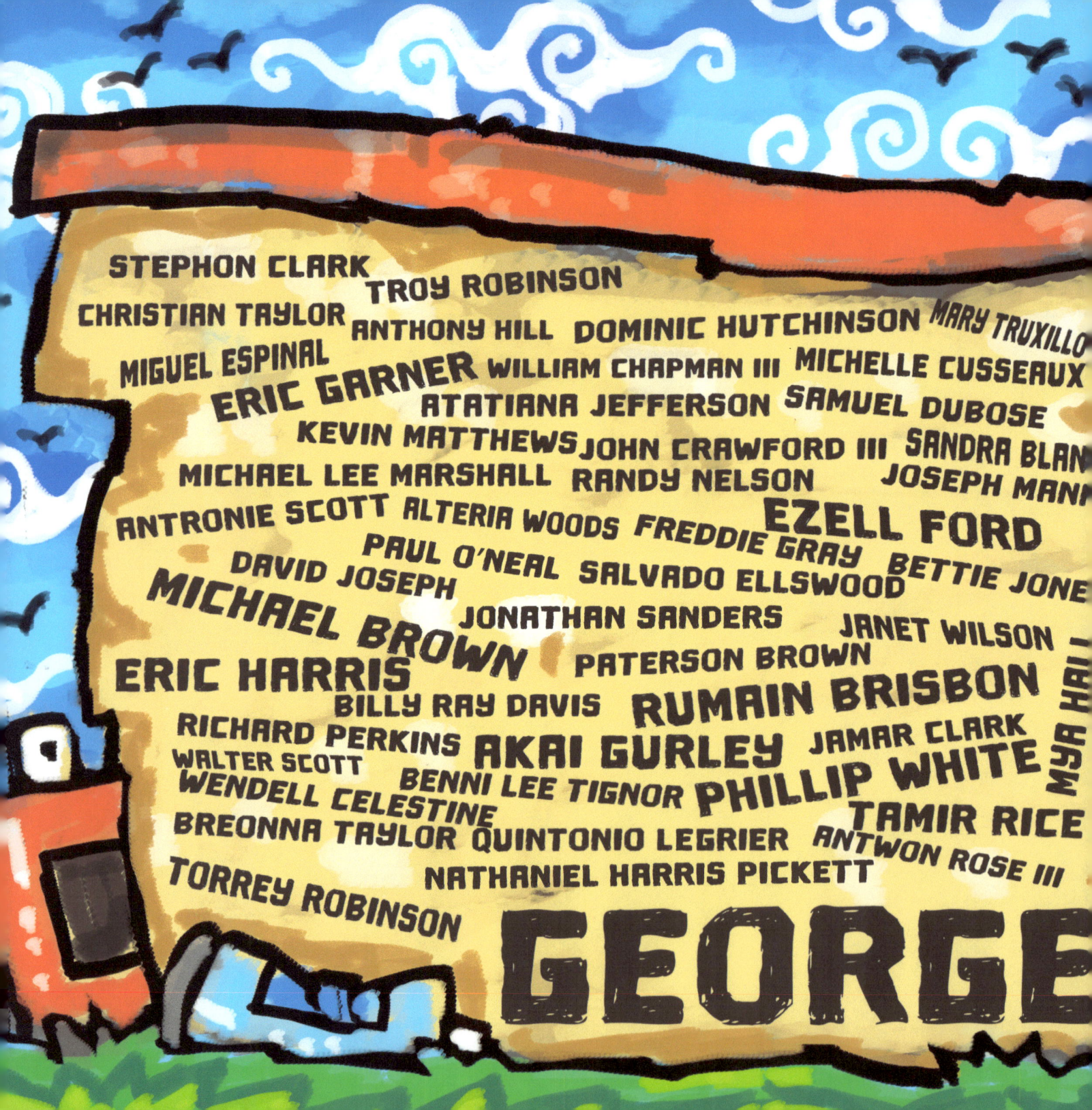

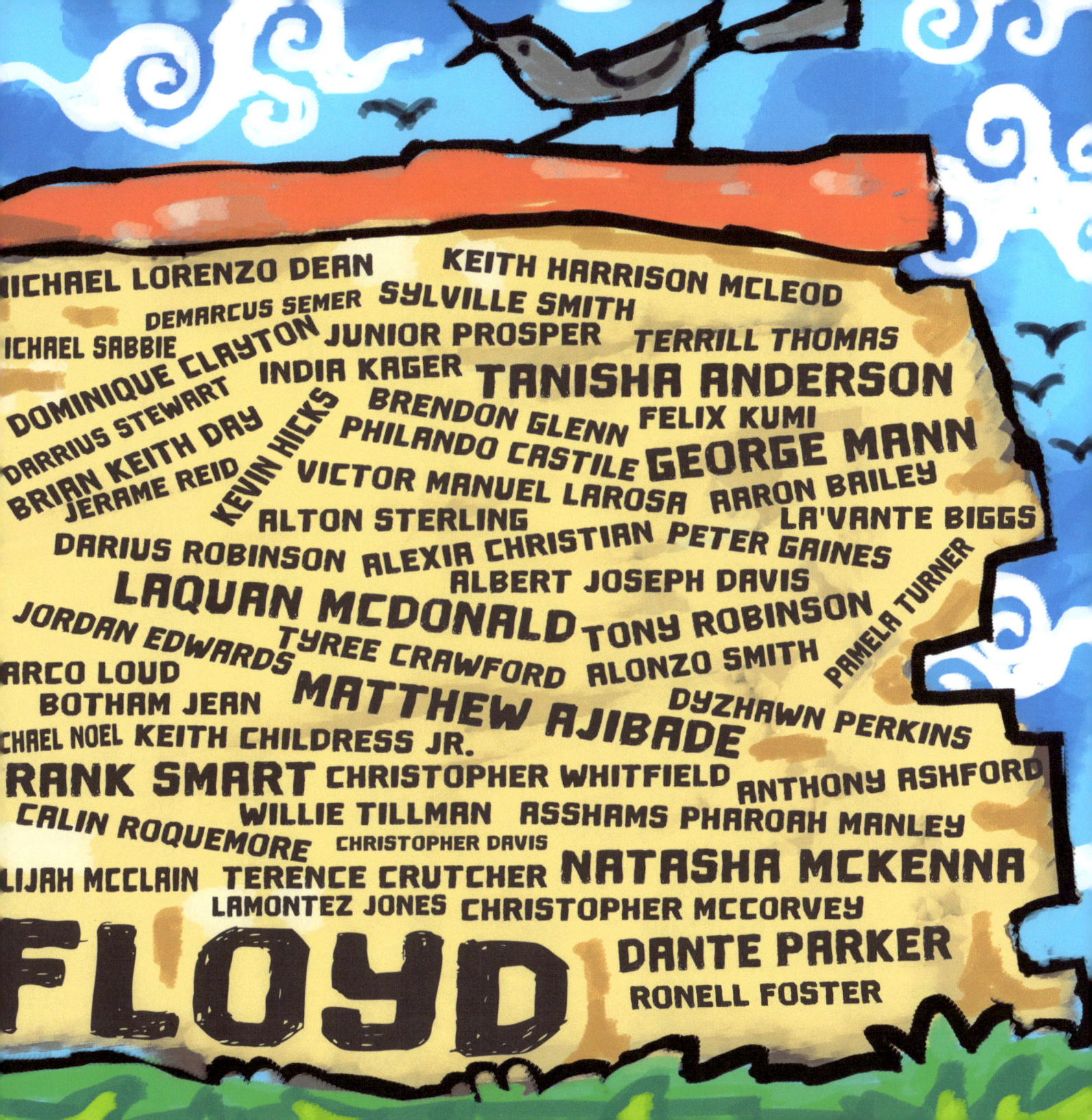

GLOSSARY

12 - Code word for narcotics officers but became a new term to describe all police.

CRIB - A house, or place where you stay.

DIP - To leave or to go.

GO HARD - To do something without worrying about consequences.

HOMIE - A close friend, someone that looks out for your well being.

PROBABLE CAUSE - Reasonable grounds (for making a search, pressing a charge, etc.).

SHOT GUN (SHOTTY) - Passenger in front seat.

SKREETS - The streets

TRAP - Mouth

WARRANT - Is a piece of paper that is signed by a judicial officer. It should have your name, address, and the reason why a search is necessary.

WHIP/WHIPPING - A car/driving a car.

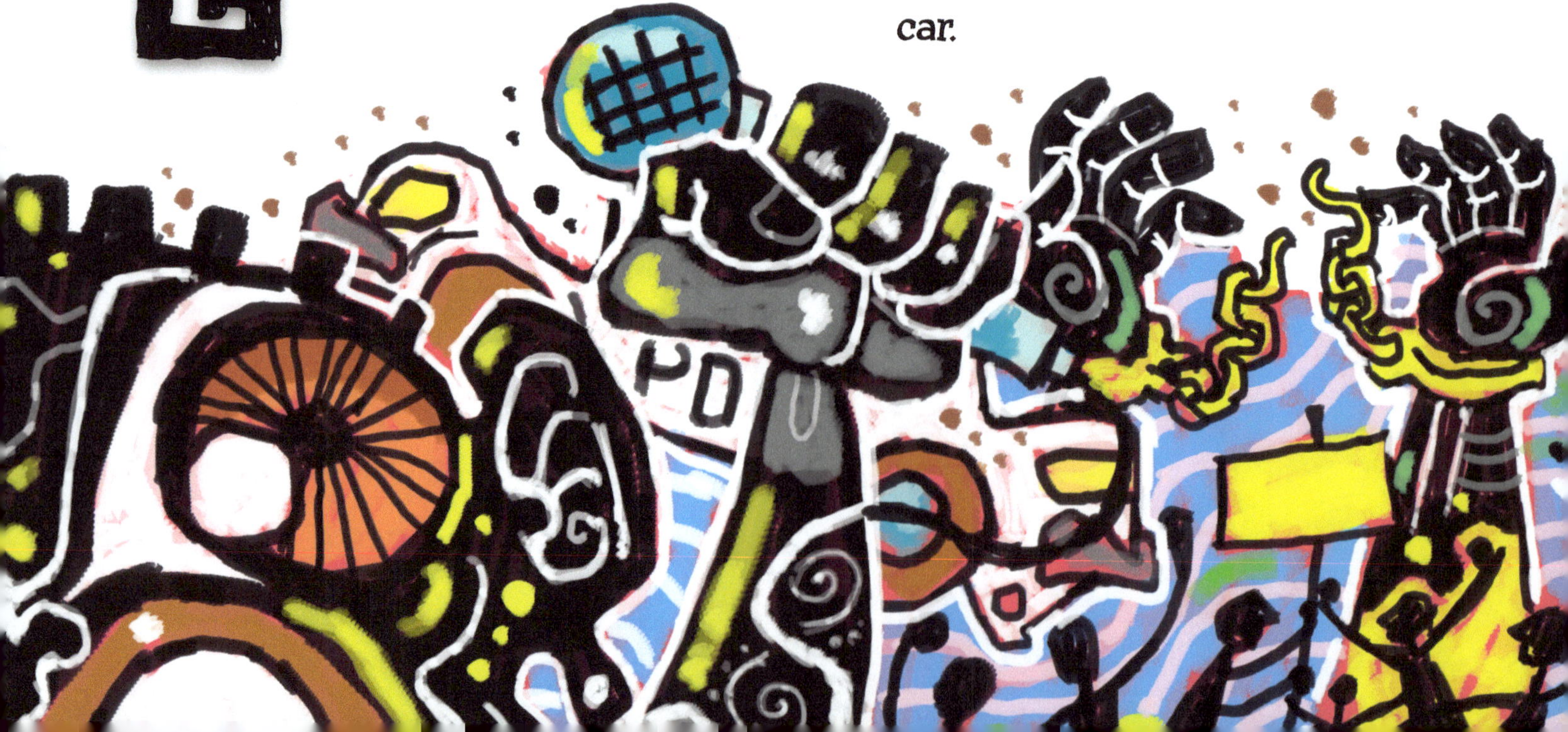

THE FIRST AMENDMENT - Is a part of the United States Bill of Rights that protects freedoms like freedom of speech, freedom of religion, freedom of assembly, freedom of the press, and right to petition.

THE FOURTH AMENDMENT - Is a part of the United States Bill of Rights and it prevents unreasonable searches and seizures and requires any search warrant to be sanctioned by a judicial officer and supported by probable cause.

NO KNOCK WARRANT - Is a warrant issued by a judge that allows TWELVE to bust in yo spot without letting you know! TWELVE might identify themselves before they bust in. The Judge gives them the warrant.

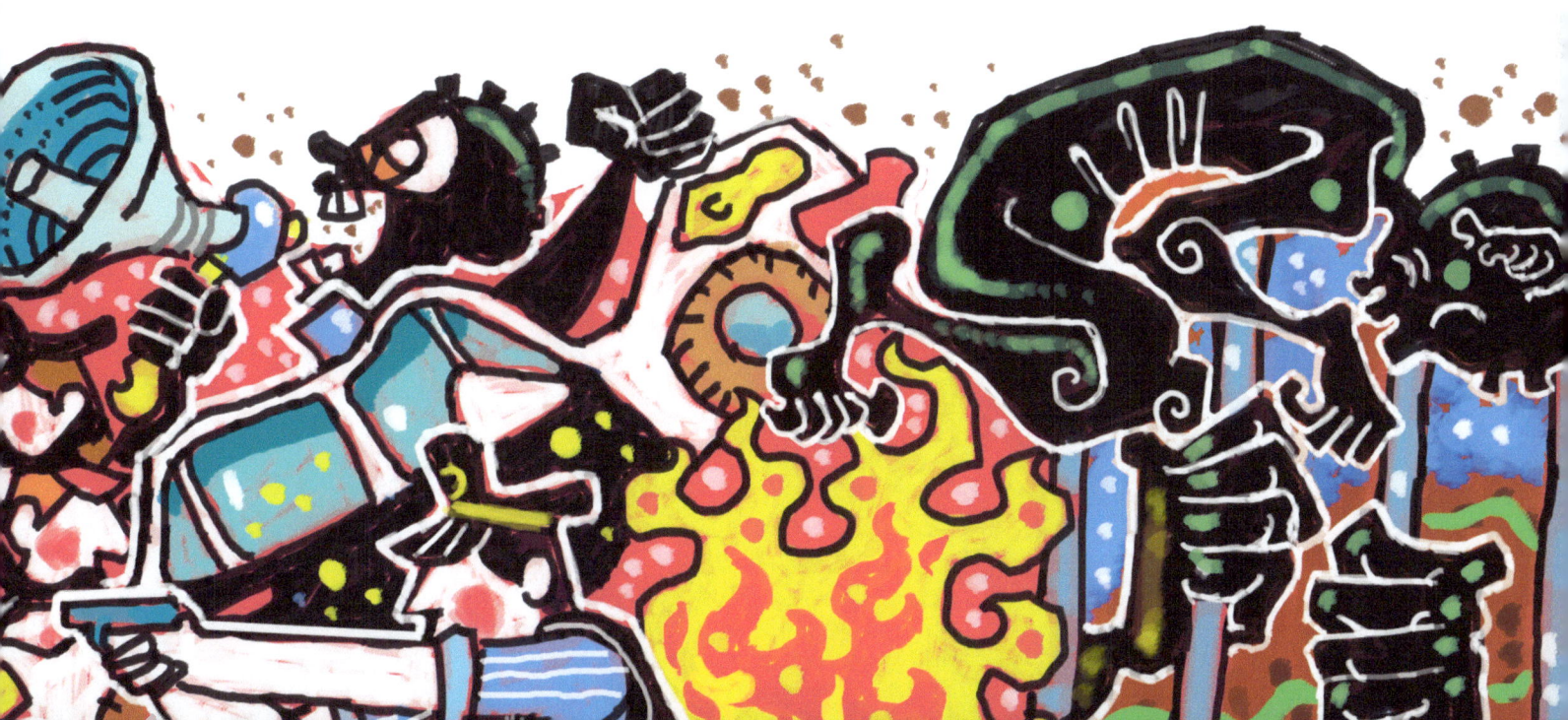